D1299970

Heart at Work

Mary,
Your open heart
touches me
and all you meet.
Cynthia Heelan
6/26/14

Heart at Work

STORIES ABOUT SPEAKING FROM THE HEART AT WORK

CYNTHIA MARY HEELAN

authorHOUSE®

AuthorHouse™
1663 Liberty Drive
Bloomington, IN 47403
www.authorhouse.com
Phone: 1-800-839-8640

© 2012 by Cynthia Mary Heelan. All rights reserved.

No part of this book may be reproduced, stored in a retrieval system, or transmitted by any means without the written permission of the author.

Published by AuthorHouse   09/04/2012

ISBN: 978-1-4772-6199-6 (sc)
ISBN: 978-1-4772-6198-9 (hc)
ISBN: 978-1-4772-6197-2 (e)

Library of Congress Control Number: 2012915088

Any people depicted in stock imagery provided by Thinkstock are models, and such images are being used for illustrative purposes only.
Certain stock imagery © Thinkstock.

Because of the dynamic nature of the Internet, any web addresses or links contained in this book may have changed since publication and may no longer be valid. The views expressed in this work are solely those of the author and do not necessarily reflect the views of the publisher, and the publisher hereby disclaims any responsibility for them.

Heart at Work

This book is a collection of Stories written by people who have explored deeply, what it means to speak plainly and openly, from the heart, with authenticity and empathy at work. Personal experience gives credence to the idea that when people speak their personal truth and respect the personal truth of others, more gets accomplished, people are more collaborative and happier in the workplace, and individuals are better served. Several of the essays in this collection are, in themselves, a collaborative effort. I interviewed individuals and wrote a draft of their essay, then they crafted the product into an essay that was more clearly their own written expression, rather than their spoken voice. The back and forth dialogue with authors was a rich experience in itself, and the essays are more powerful as a result.

Endorsements

"Heart at Work is a book needed at a time when there is a decreased premium paid to the human dimension in our workplaces and this is likely extracting a cost that's not quantified." Henry Shilling, Sr. V. P., Moody's Investors Service.

"If you want to bring your whole self to work, to live a seamless life with mind and heart aligned for the tasks before you, you will find a wise and gentle guide in *Heart at Work*. Hafiz long ago wrote: 'Love is the great work, though every heart is first an apprentice . . .'. This gem of a book brings these words to life through authentic stories that illustrate, inform and inspire the reader to create their own authentic life's work." **Henry Emmons, MD,** *Author, The Chemistry of Joy; The Chemistry of Calm; and The Chemistry of Joy Workbook: Overcoming Depression Using the Best of Brain Science, Nutrition and the Psychology of Mindfulness, Integrative Psychiatrist and Health Care Leader.*

"This collection of essays by nationally and internationally recognized leaders calls for a fundamental change in leadership and day to day practices. Anchored in solid research and seasoned by broad based personal experiences, these diverse professionals give us key principles and concrete applications that can help us do, love, and be from the inside out. It is a much needed response to the external social forces that drive us toward expedient actions that do not serve basic human needs." ***Arthur Chickering, PhD***, *Author, Encouraging Authenticity & Spirituality in Higher Education, Educational Leader.*

"*Creating for Children* by Ginna Gemmell has lessons learned that we would be wise to hold onto in today's economic environment. How you are "being"—supporting each other through work and life's challenges, having a future focus, and a positive outlook, living your companies core values, taking calculated risks, accepting costly mistakes and, impacting the environment and success. Ginna Gemmell's perspective, as well as insight from other authors in Heart at Work, is refreshing. Simple and true. A breath of fresh air." ***Blaine LeRoy***, *Executive Coach, Business Consultant.*

"It's so rich to hear the stories of people from different occupations and how they came to live in a place of connection with their true self." **Laurie Erickson***, Spiritual Director, Minneapolis, MN*

Also by Cynthia Heelan (with Gail Mellow)

Minding the Dream: Process and Practice in the American
Community College

Contents

> A letter in the form of poetry describes the heart of a teacher who longs for all the principles for which this books stands. Written during a writing retreat titled: Writing to Put the Heart at Rest, this loving teacher who feels robbed of joy, describes that for which she longs, a principal who speaks from the heart, laughter, deep, meaningful conversation, a welcoming spirit!

> On the journey to speaking from the heart and being creative, it helps to understand how often we act from a place that is based on "should and could" rather than discerning what we know in our hearts to be right. This chapter offers a way to look at an individual's inner life and suggests its potential impact on our professional lives.

For some people, it may be helpful to hear more from the experts who write about finding, losing and reclaiming heart. This chapter discusses the journey to finding heart along with supportive citations.

Brian Delate's Vietnam experience and his experience as a writer, an actor and as a film maker are empowered by his own personal growth. His film, Soldier's Heart, the Civil War term for PTSD, brings together his self knowledge, his willingness to share, and his skill in the art of film.

As Founder and Artistic Director and President of Battery Dance Company, Jonathan Hollander lives in and speaks from his heart in a very special way. His choreography, as his life of the spirit evolves, becomes increasingly a co-creation with his dancers. These opportunities allow for dance experiences that move the hearts of kings and children, and audiences worldwide.

A former Manager of New Product Research at Fisher Price Toys, explores the rich corporate creativity and productivity resulting when people are able to speak honestly and playfully.

Integrative, holistic medical practitioner, Bill Manahan, MD, describes the difference between traditional western medicine and integrative/holistic medical practice. Bill is presently involved in efforts to transform America's health care system and the healers involved in that system. He believes that we need a new model of health care that is based on a partnership model, the pursuit of wellness, community collaboration, social connection, and assumption of personal responsibility.

All employees in an organization could have opportunities to provide leadership. When we understand more about our authentic inner core, we act differently. This chapter discusses the importance of this understanding and some of the results of making a commitment to lead and follow authentically and from our hearts.

Winner of the coveted Baldrige Award in higher education, President Emeritus of Richland College of the Dallas

Community College District, is living proof that lives formed by listening to an inner guide can come together to co-create a quality oriented and productive organization.

This chapter is a Former Chancellor's exploration of individual and collective efforts at Maricopa Community College to create an organization where all of its members seek and find integration between their inner life and the work they do. He proposes that the consequence of such a path would be an ever more powerful, and ever more dynamic college.

Appreciative Inquiry is a practical approach to organizational planning and solution finding. The process invites each member of an organization to share a success story with colleagues. Personal stories become the basis for creating a college-wide scenario that builds on success. This scenario evolves into a plan providing an opportunity for every person to contribute to and co-create the future of their organization.

Staff members who have participated in renewal and wholeness retreats find themselves more connected to their colleagues, they gain confidence in their competence, find new resources to use in their work. They build trust in themselves and in their workplace as a community.

The final chapter provides a diagram of how internal growth, heart at work, new ideas, new solutions, new productivity, and new and happy customers creates a new prototype. This is, in a few words, the "so what," the "Take Away" of the Chapters contained in this book

List of Illustrations

Preface to Heart at Work
by Cynthia Heelan PhD

There are books describing the importance of authenticity, of speaking plainly and openly, from the heart, at work, and then ultimately influencing decision-making processes and services to clients. Most of those books are written by theorists and philosophers. Few are by practitioners who also EXPERIENCE the transformation, not only within themselves and in a more holistic workplace, but in the clients they serve.

During my years as a college president and since, facilitating dialogue on college campuses, I have observed people who are allowed to speak plainly and who participate in decision-making. I have seen the energy in a room of 500 people soar from low morale to high expectations as employees focus on some story of a peak success in their organization and then work together with a shared sense of purpose to expand that success and co-create an even more successful future. I have seen resulting quality programs, creative action and inspiration spreading throughout the organization. One college faculty and staff amazed themselves when they read the vision they'd written for the next five years. "We've never used words like this before: social justice, commitment to innovation." These words and the concepts they represented emerged because the college had listened to every single person who chose to speak from their heart about what was important at their college; and plan authors had used everyone's words as captured during a large group process.

This experience at work has a powerful impact on services provided and on clients served. Richland College, a community college in the Dallas Community College District, where exploring one's inner self is part of every employee's signed contract, won the national Baldridge Award for Higher Education, for their educational excellence as well as for high institutional morale. Richland College President, Steve Mittelstet and I have worked together and have had conversations about dialogue at work, and I have talked with professionals from fields other than education. These colleagues all have similar stories to tell: When people work on their own inner transformation they are more able to create an environment where people feel safe to speak freely, from their hearts, and eventually productivity and creativity increase, and service to clients increases exponentially.

Why is this experience so rare—if only leaders understood. When people learn to, and feel free to, speak from an authentic place, without fear, their workplace becomes inspired by shared purpose; it is marked by extraordinary quality and productivity. In this book, several practitioner/authors describe and tell actual stories about their own work. A toy manufacturer describes the connection to their customer, children, through play. A soldier describes how his struggle to survive PTSD, enables his ability to support other soldiers. An artistic director and choreographer reveals the transformation that occurs when dancers share in the creative process. College presidents describe their increased ability to open their hearts and then increased staff and student success as people become more engaged. Medical doctors describe how their own personal transformation impacted their medical practices. Authors describe the ways their inner work and then meaningful sharing with colleagues, results in innovation, creativity and positive action, including better service to clients. The authors of Heart at Work want this experience to become the norm.

Interest in This Topic

Increasing numbers of today's workers seek a sense of deeper purpose in their work lives, yet not many organizations engage in the kind of dialogue described above. Too often when people leave for work in the morning; they leave their personal truth lying at the bottom of their hearts, or at their kitchen table, and they close the door on them. At the same time, every organization, whether it is an educational institution, a medical center, a corporation, a family, an art gallery or a dance or film company, experiences the pressure to be creative, productive and effective. Too many of these organizations do not understand that the most important thing they can do to be more creative, productive and effective as an organization, is to unleash the truth hidden at the bottom of the hearts of their employees. This unleashing can be initiated by simply providing opportunities for people to sort through those things most important to them and then dialogue about them with their colleagues. The *Heart at Work* addresses this need.

Gender inclusion is important for me, and so throughout this book, I have chosen to randomly use gender pronouns.

Acknowledgements

I want to acknowledge my teachers, John Lincoln, Charles Elias, and Christine Schenk. My fellow students in the Chris Technique, my teachers and colleagues in the Center for Renewal and Wholeness in Higher Eduction and in the Center for Courage and Renewal. You have been loving co-travelers on a very important path to trusting my own inner wisdom. The loving and attentive members of my writing group, Mary Downs and Susan Bruss, helped to craft this book into a worthy publication.

A Letter To My Principal

by Diane Petteway

My dear instructional leader,

Speaking the truth in love,
Your eyes gather data like lasers.
Numbers are more important than feelings.
You flash your smile—but it does not reach your eyes.

Do you lead from fear?

What gives you life?

Your rhythm is the essence of a river.

It all depends on faith.
It all depends on wonder.

The trick is finding the opening.

When a heart is closed, where does one find the small door in?

I shut down around you.
I allow you to rob me of my joy.

I need a leader who can lead from the heart.

Laughter.
Conversation.
Deep, meaningful conversation.
Being "in flow" . . . . uninterrupted time . . . .
A welcoming spirit

Absence of flow limits me . . . .
The essence of flow is why I teach.

I am anxious to move to action.
I am embarrassed that you are not visible.
I have realized how disengaged you are.

What will emerge from this?

I don't know my decision until I hear your response.

I am tired of writing about you.

Finding My Heart, The Work before Going to Work

by Cynthia Heelan PhD

My personal journey to speaking with authenticity, from the heart at work, is permeated with experiences that frustrated and discouraged me, and broke my heart, bit by bit. Many groups and individuals describe a source for authentic behavior. The Quakers name it inner teacher, Alcoholics Anonymous calls it higher power, Christians call it soul or spirit or grace, and Thomas Merton called it the true self. Each group's intention is to identify a basic self that functions at a higher level than ego or identity or personality. One broken bit of my heart came to me, when I searched for a creative approach to strategic planning for my college.

The college was developing a plan for upgrading technology hardware and software. Colleges were being brought to their knees by the simple act of installing a new software system, and ours was a legacy system, no longer creating updates. Conferences on survival appeared at Educause, Academic Computing Meetings and the National Association of College and University Business

3

Officers. As 2000 and Y2K approached, and with every disaster article I read, I felt more panic. I spoke with a consultant I trusted. I wanted the college to go beyond surviving Y2K and getting students registered and people paid. I wanted exciting academic approaches to teaching students and ways to improve student learning. I felt the planning committee was bogged down in administrative details and student registration. So, I sought new and exciting ways to plan, thinking that might jog people's minds.

In a book about vision by Robert Fritz, *The Path of Least Resistance.* Fritz notes the importance of keeping current reality in mind while envisioning a more innovative future. He equates the tension between the two, as that of a rubber band pulling on both reality and vision at the same time. It's important to value that tension and to stand, consciously, in the middle, while gradually moving toward the vision and letting go of less satisfying remnants of reality. I'm a rabid reader, avidly influenced by what I read, when it makes sense, to me. This often resulted in, me, pushing new ideas at work.

The creative tension model for strategic planning seemed perfect, to me, for my meeting with the technology committee. My voice probably vibrated with excitement as I introduced this, yet another new idea. I introduced the concept to the Technology Planning Committee. "Look, at this diagram. (I had my newsprint already posted, ready to draw!) Can you visualize a NEW reality in addition to simply replacing the current reality with new software?" Disgruntled staff members looked at me with disbelief as I attempted to guide them in this new and foreign direction. They looked like the rubber band I drew on the newsprint—taut, inflexible and uncompromising. This was a new response to my ideas.

My very long honeymoon period as a college president, and its honeyed goodness of approval, naturally and gradually diffused, and the tight response became more frequent. I increasingly faced a table of taut rubber bands, and I found my teeth clenched, my hands gripping a chair; I was my own taut rubber band. I heard a lack of support for ideas as a stiffened roar of rejection. As I sat with this feeling of rebuff, I discerned something was missing, and that something, was in me. I could feel the energy seeping from me like air from a tire, and a can of "Fix a Flat" wasn't going to work for repairs. I slowly realized, I was missing an ability to affirm myself.

As I read further in Fritz's book, he, a musician, described how this planning process was used by artists of all genres. He emphasized how a painter might step up to a canvas with a general vision for a painting, but not know exactly, the first brush stroke. A musician could sit at the piano and know, basically, what a new composition would say, and not know the first note. The artist, trusts her inner self to act, to create, to lay down the first color or note or word.

I could see how this related to developing a strategic plan for the college. I envisioned us in a brainstorming process that might open us to be in touch with wisdom in us and among us. Exploring the college's future and creative tension could take us to a preferable, more innovative future.

Fritz, eventually gave visioning a dramatic twist. He moved his work away from creating an organizational vision to disclosing how artists use the process for planning their arts, but not for their inner lives. So, Fritz wrote his book as a guide to a personal visioning; applying the artistic process to trusting the inner self to act and to create, daily, one's own, inner, life.

Attempting to deal with my energy loss, as well as Y2K, I sought these ideas for my own stretched rubber band, my flat tire. I would follow Fritz's advice for my inner life; little did I know the disquietude I would find rumbling in my heart. At the same time, little did I know the disquietude the college would experience as we moved forward to resolve Y2K issues.

Fritz suggested we make statements on a regular basis about what we want in our lives. I began to say several times daily, "I choose to be true to myself." I felt confident I knew my true self, my heart. I was honest, caring, creative, hard working and assertive. I guess I thought I would just become more that way. After making the statement for a while, however, information I didn't like, came to me. I became aware of a big black ball in my throat, and a knot in my stomach. I realized I didn't know my true self—heart eluded me. "Where did this black ball and knot originate?" "How long had I had them and didn't pay attention to them?" As I sat with these questions, it occurred to me, the self I knew was somewhat a shell. It was supported by approval, positive feedback and respect I received from colleagues and friends. The gradual loss of adulation at the college was affecting my physical body.

My heart cracked open a bit, and I became open to new information. I could hear my anxiety and and fear during times of stress and sensed it bred anxiety in those around me. I noticed how my physical health and mental attitude were influenced by the coffee I drank (my version of Fix a Flat?) and the food I ate and the way I internalized criticism or lack of positive response. I determined true heart was too demanding. I needed help. I found the perfect guide, a coach, who turned out to be part coach and part spiritual director. He helped me explore my lost heart.

Losing Heart

I asked my coach, "Why is it so difficult to access my heart some of the time. Where does my heart go?" My guide asked me questions about my past, and I began to think about the times when my heart "showed up" and it was not welcome.

As a child I was sassy; I contradicted my parents, I needed to be right. To my parents, I was seldom right. I was willful. I devoted a lot of my childhood to sitting on a chair in a corner. I also spent fifteen minutes every evening, bent over that chair. With knees and heart chafing, distractedly repeating with Archbishop Fulton J. Sheen, the truly mysterious radio rosary. My devout, Irish Catholic mother wept and ranted with frustration at my imperfections. Once, mother was so disheartened with me, she packed my suitcase, placing my seven year old shoes on top of the bag. When my father came home for lunch, he would be taking me to reform school. I felt doomed. I was beyond my mother's ability to cope. By the time Dad came home for lunch, however, the bag and shoes had disappeared, and mother was onto something else.

In elementary school, I finished my work in record time and then rambled around the classroom. Even though desks were lashed together and fixed to the floor, I could still find a way to wander and chat amiably with classmates. I inevitably heard the tight, shrill of exasperated Sister Irene yanking me back to my desk. She inflicted extra work to keep me busy, awarded me low grades in deportment, then delivered me to Irish exasperation, which did not exclude the wrath of God, the hand, or the plea. Eventually, I found myself stuttering. My erudite Chapter on the Typewriter became a series of t-t-t-t-t's, much to Sister Irene's chagrin, my classmate's amusement, and my horror.

As an adult at work, I took the Myers Briggs profile test and learned, despite my Irish Catholic upbringing, I still had managed to become an ENTJ, the nickname for which is field marshall or Sherman tank! I was called on the carpet for talking too much, for acting like I knew it all, when, to me, I was spontaneously donating my ideas. I seemed to others to be trying to act like a boss. One day, at a new job, I was participant in a meeting to design a new program. This was an area where I had moderate experience, and I immediately piped up with a list of ideas for pursuing new programs. I am sure my voice crackled with purpose, as I snapped out ideas; spilling my heart. What my boss saw was an over confident and high-handed newbie who spurted "know it all." He later came into my office and said, "I need you to know I am the boss here, and I don't need any help being boss." A consultant confided to me later, that I needed, essentially, to learn when to keep my head down and my mouth shut. He then taught me how to make others think my ideas were theirs. I worked mightily to change my behavior, so I could be a successful college administrator.

I finally learned to adapt to fit into my parents' image of a good girl, and to institutional demands for competent leadership. I dealt with the threat of rejection by shifting between the public world of my role and the hidden world of my heart. I began to wear a mask to

7

cover my anxiety, my vulnerability. I lost my voice. Not the ability to speak, the ability to speak from my heart. My anxiety became a black lump in my throat and in my gut, that I lugged around with me from job to job and relationship to relationship. So this is where my heart goes! This is why I get so anxious when things don't go my way and when I am criticized.

Reclaiming Heart

With the assistance of my coach, and a lot of reading material, I moved toward understanding true heart was deeper—a more essential self—a self that emerged if I could breathe deeply and listen—trust myself to be guided by it. He guided me step by step in this process.

Breathing Into Internal Spaces

My coach invited me to see and feel where my body felt anxiety. I easily identified my throat and my gut. He taught me to catch myself in the act of feeling anxious. At first, I had to do this many times in a day. I would sit at my desk, my stomach in a knot, throat constricted, close my eyes and begin to breathe. I would feel the tight feelings until I felt as though I would burst, it hurt so much. I would keep feeling it, without distracting myself with other thoughts, then acknowledge my inability to rid myself of the anxiety by myself and breathe into the feelings. Surprisingly, acknowledging the physical feeling and breathing into that space, allowed the anxiety to dissipate, and I would be flooded with feelings of well-being, openness, and a loving feeling for myself and my colleagues. Gradually my feelings of anxiety subsided, my internal rubber band released. What a surprise. My attempt to stand in the tension instead of ignoring it or running from it, allowed my heart to break open instead of falling apart. I remembered Robert Fritz: if I hold the tension of my internal, clenched rubber band without pushing, I can gradually move toward my vision of being true to myself. I felt increasingly able to guide decisions without doubt, to be open to criticism, to deal with the daily conflicts that arose in a more peaceful and integrated manner. I felt a solidity, a definiteness, groundedness and greater kindness, strength, joy and warmth that was different from my usual fire and excitability.

Others noticed it too. One dean, her shoulders slumped, would slip into my office and collapse into a chair near my desk, "I just want to sit here awhile and absorb your energy" she would say.

I could hear a new harmony singing in my heart without the usual chorus of approval from outside myself. I discerned an inner awareness. I brought more heart to work, and I created space for staff to bring theirs to the planning table. To solve the Y2K concern, I created a search committee at the college to interview consultant groups who could assist us to select an appropriate software program and to ensure we were excellent at both administrative and instructional practices. The committee recommended the top three consultants, and, similar to other positions, I selected the final candidate. The college was not happy with my final selection, even though the group was among the top three. My inner work made it possible for me to withstand the criticism as well as spend time talking and working through the effort with various groups.

The Value of Not Knowing

There are other supports to helping ones heart to stay open and to open more instead of breaking apart. Another thing I learned about cracking myself open to hear my heart, is being able to say to myself, "I don't know." Admitting I have forgotten who I am, what is important and not important, or how things ought to turn out, creates a quiet mind and can allow for a transformation of my state of mind and heart.

We created a leadership program that focused not so much on doing as on Being, and this included physical feats that terrified me, like rappelling. I am terror stricken of heights and generally, I am not adept at physical activities. Indeed, I was always, sadly, the last one chosen for any team!

Silently and with serenity, my colleague Colorado natives who rappelled for fun on weekends, eased down the wall. When it was my turn, I crumpled onto a rock, high above a wall in Leadville, Colorado, and sobbed. The Colorado desert all around me, clogged my heart with its aridity. I felt embarrassed, lonely, a failure. Before me flashed memories of a little girl in brown stockings, grimacing as the first to be captured in Red Rover and shrugging as the last to be chosen, (with a sigh) for the softball team.

Suddenly, remembering my work with my coach, I acknowledged to myself my fear and failing, and my total lack of knowledge and experience in rappelling. Holding the tension for myself, I felt deeply, the dread, apprehension and foreboding of that wall, and I sucked in a deep, deep breath, thinking to myself, "So this is what it means to "suck it up." As I held the tension and breathed, I unexpectedly began to feel open to new possibilities for myself. I felt a kind of peace and calm, perhaps, attempting the wall could be possible.

Inching toward the wall, and listening to the Outward Bound instructor coach me step by step, I gingerly planted my heels against the edge of the wall. The instructor guided me to eye the thick rope safely wound around a tree and my teacher's waist, and I did **not** look down as she described the person below who also had a rope around me. I tentatively lowered one foot down the cliff. Recalling Robert Fritz inspired me, "Maybe, when I start down this cliff, what I need will come to me." I relinquished flat ground and lowered the other foot. I found myself taking one step after another, all the way down the cliff. When I reached solid ground, I once again, fell into a heap of relief and dissolved, again, into tears. The acute fear of not knowing how to get down the wall, breathing into it, moving through the fear and believing what I needed would guide each foot, grazed my heart and opened yet another fissure. My internal rubber band held the tension once again, and moved me gently toward my vision of an open and authentic heart.

At the college, I became increasingly able to stop worrying about conflicts I would have to face or problems that needed solving. I became increasingly able to approach conflicts with both feet on the ground and accept that if I could acknowledge that I didn't know what should happen next, if I took one step after another and trusted I had everything I needed to work with others to resolve issues, we could resolve them.

Physical Activities

Athletic or physical body activities help me toward heart reclamation. In my Yoga classes, I am invited to hold a position or engage in a movement until it hurts so much I think I have to rest. If I can open my mind and my heart and believe I have it in me to continue for one more second, and then one more and then another, and if I keep observing the ache and breathe into the source of the ache and pain, a new energy arises and I can continue on in the position or movement with ease. I then feel a sense of wholeness, elation, expansiveness, peace and openness all throughout my body and my spirit.

The Yoga Center at Kripalu suggests we think of living our lives as "Yoga off the mat." In other words, I've learned to feel the depression, the anger, the anxiety, the fear, the vulnerability, or the doubt in the fullness and depth of the feeling, until it feels so painful I hunger for a distraction. Then, If I keep an open and loving heart and breathe into the physical place where it aches, my heart, will take over and fill me with the same sense of wholeness, peace and openness I feel in our physical body when I pass through physical barriers. As I do this more, I have a greater awareness and am able to live more fully from my heart.

I have a friend whose daughter is a marathon runner. When she gets to mile 23, she describes feeling helpless to continue. She feels the agony of throbbing, blistered feet, and she wants to quit. Yet she wants to finish even more and has a vision for finishing. So she acknowledges her pain, observes its impact, and then takes one more step and one more step and one more; she keeps breathing into her aching limbs and she feels a new energy source arise and take her to mile 26.

Conclusion

After many of these experiences, yoga, breathing, and the total not knowing of rappelling down a very high cliff, and the support (belaying) I found in my colleagues, I discovered people at work were saying I was different. A board member asked me, "What happened at that leadership program? People are talking about your change." My sense of humor was more evident, I was less cautious and my heart was just plain more open to all. More people opened their own heart and spoke freely about their ideas and wants.

A.H. Almaas, psychiatrist and author says, when we finally accept and feel our helplessness in the face of our anger or our fear or our loss of our heart, and when we experience it in a totally open and impartial manner, the deficient and tight emptiness loses its power and changes into a vast spaciousness. Not knowing involves giving up the conviction that we know what to do, and that we are inadequate because we cannot do it. Breathing fills us with new energy and resolve and spirit.

Heart never abandons us; we abandon it. We can reclaim our birth given gift of heart and learn again to taste and to share, the mellow, exciting, sweet and fleshy harvest of inner work.

Finding Heart, The Work Before Work: the Experts

By Cynthia Heelan PhD

The Organizational Chess Game of squeeze and squirm has all too often been our experience in organizational life. Often during my career, I have been pressured to be political and to use my power to influence others in the manner of a Chess game. I tried always to resist that approach and consequently, I have been squeezed, and I have squirmed quite a bit myself. It took me a long time to accept that I was no Chess player! My approach to politics has been to build relationships and to trust that others, when faced with this trust, will be trustworthy. This is not always true. When relationship building didn't work, and others waited for me to make a followup move to an attack, I would blame myself and then go straight to stress related illness. This stress not only affected me, it affected all the people with whom I worked. It affects all the people in every organization when they observe the Chess Game of moving in on players, picking off players, and cornering people in ways that are demeaning and punishing.

There needs to be another approach to organizational life. There IS another approach. It is to be present to our own heart, to speak openly about the truth and to create space for others in the organization to do the same. Ultimately we can improve service to clients. The point of this book is to give examples of how to do this. The first step is to connect to our own heart, to understand heart or Essential Self, to re-find it if we have lost it, and to nurture on-going "Heart Support."

Living from our heart suggests far more than sincerity. Yet, going beyond sincere is critical to productive and inspired organizations. An open heart evolves from a place in ourselves much deeper than many of us ever venture. Parker Palmer thinks of the authentic person as one who is willing to explore self—the total self—filled with both light and shadow, and then has the courage to stay open when things are most difficult. Authenticity among leaders, staff and constituents creates an environment leading to creativity, growth, mission fulfillment and culture transformation. A heart open in this way releases a continuous flow of rich inner life: outward to influence action, and experiences flow inward, to affect inner development.

The Importance of an Open Heart

Connecting to our heart, allowing our inner and our external actions to be in continuous connection is a joyous experience when we are in our "flow" so to speak, or when we feel energetic, secure and positive. It is a frightening thing when we suspect there are aspects to our inner selves that aren't so healthy, when we get an inkling or learn we're acting out of our shadow, or false self, when we sense our shadow is falling on those in our presence. On those days when facing my shadow is really difficult, or when I wake up in the middle of the night thinking about some mistake I've made, I ask myself, is it really so important to do this work? Maybe I've gone far enough down this path! Then I remember (or am reminded by external experience) if I don't do this work I leave behind me, in my wake, a stream of hurt feelings, confusion, frustration and annoyance for those left standing in my shadow. Finding ways to make our inner flow and our outer actions as one is actually crucial for good leadership, for truly serving clients, and for healthy organizational life.

The Mobius Strip is a metaphor for inner reflection and

outer action

A metaphor for this inner flow and outer action, the Mobius Strip can be used to visualize this journey to an open heart. To visualize the Mobius Strip, take a strip of paper and instead of taping the two ends together smoothly, give one end a twist. Tape the two ends together. There is suddenly no outside nor inside on the Mobius Strip. The two sides keep blending into one another—the inside becomes the outside—the outside becomes the inside. The point of the Mobius Strip is it gives us a visual for allowing whatever is inside us to continually flow outward to touch the world, for good or for ill—and for allowing whatever is outside us to continually flow inward to touch our inner selves, for good or ill. The internal/external flow of the Mobius strip is life; we create our reality with who we are—with our internal / external flow. Do we create a reality that is authentic, open,vulnerable and vital, or one that is false and closed?

Thinking of the Mobius Strip is helpful to me when I feel tempted to close my heart: to hide my vulnerability or my enthusiasm or even my strengths at times when I feel they might not be welcome. This visual image also helps me when I feel lured to go along with an action I do not support or when I'm tempted to be intolerant or grandiose or too meek in a leadership setting. The visual image of the Mobius also is a reminder that my inner life is guided by more than my willpower; there is another flow within me that is a source for my open heart or authenticity, my Personal Essence.

What is Heart or Personal Essence

Many groups and individuals describe a source for authentic behavior. The Quakers name it inner teacher, Alcoholics Anonymous calls it higher power, Christians call it soul or spirit or grace, and Thomas Merton called it the true self. Each group's intention is to identify a basic self that functions at a higher level than ego or identity or personality. A.H. Almaas is a physicist, psychologist and teacher who created the Diamond Approach to growth. He calls it Personal Essence and refers to it as true existence, a presence, Being that can help us discern human and personal life. It is the truly integrated and developed human being. Our personality or ego is only a dim reflection of Personal Essence. In this book, when we refer to heart, we are thinking of this concept of Personal Essence. It all sounds very complex, and understanding Personal Essence, or heart, and then living from it is a life long journey, and everyone's journey begins somewhere.

My journey, like most of us, began some time ago. It took an interesting turn when I had been a college president for about five years; I read a book about vision by Robert Fritz called The Path of Least Resistance. I read this book to learn more about creating a vision with my college, and soon discovered that Fritz, a musician, described the creative process used by artists of all genres. I

17

describe how this book and the suggestions Fritz makes influenced me and my behavior, in the previous Chapter, Finding My Heart.

We Lose Touch with our Heart

It's difficult to live from heart, to be authentic all the time. It turns out, the very basis for our authentic life is different from what we work all our lives to develop. From the beginning, we adapt to fit into our parents' image of a good girl, or society's expectation of a good person, or to institutional demands for competent leadership (think the Chess Game) or effective teaching. We all find ourselves adapting to the demands of "reality" in order to be found acceptable and ready for our station in life. In this way our personality or identity evolves. We leave behind our openness, integrity, resilience, forthrightness and respond to the pressure to play someone else, when the true self starts to feel threatened. We deal with the threat of rejection by moving daily between the public world of our job and the hidden world of our heart. We wear a mask and an armor to cover our anxiety, our vulnerability, or our warmth.

We Are Born Authentic

It is often said that children are a good source for identifying the true self because they are still close to their natural gifts. We are born with a heart that contains our uniqueness, a knowledge of who we are, why we are here, and how we are related to others. Many of us abandon that knowledge as we grow up, but that heart never abandons us.

My sister has endless delightful stories of her eight grandchildren between the ages of 1 and 11. She tells stories of children creating and singing songs that come from their open hearts, stories of physical exuberance and flowing movements, total honesty and clarity ("Gary, what's that in your belly" to the portly uncle). She describes children's ability to select outrageous clothing combinations that reflect their colorful imagination. She revels in their openly affectionate and loving natures. We do seem to be born this way, and then, we lose it.

My coach taught me this too. We are not really born with our egos, our personality; we **learn** this self image. We are born into the realm of heart, this sense of heart is never totally lost, and actually manifests in children in predictable and supportable ways even though it is not fully developed.

It is true that awareness of heart is lost in the process of developing our personality and our ego, but by understanding this, we can actually remember in detail the process of our forgetting our true self. We can remember, understand and undo this forgetting, retrieve what has been suppressed and open the way for growing into true maturity and for being grounded in our own true heart. Like the air seeping from a tire, perhaps losing energy is a symptom of corrosion on our rim. We may need to do a bit of cleansing and resealing, and then rebalance our ourselves. We can do this if we are willing to feel, observe and name our shadows, instead of trying to numb them. The pain of feeling and naming our corrosion, our dark side will open our heart, and draw us out, toward healing and more authentic behavior and ultimately toward greater vitality for those around us. If, in this way, we can find our way back to our childlike selves, filled with heart, we can find ourselves teaching and leading, doctoring and nursing, acting, film making and creating from our inner self like the artist described by Robert Fritz. We can create from our heart. We can rely on an intelligence that shows up as an appropriate response to the needs in whatever situation we find ourselves. When love is needed, our heart can show up in the form of Love which guides us to act in loving ways; when strength is needed, it can be present for us, guiding us to act with strength and vitality. Heart is a completely non-selfish, flow of our essential nature as it unfolds naturally and authentically.

The "naturalness" of the internal flow and external action, is the way of the child, the Mobius Strip, the way of our heart. It never abandons us; we abandon it. We can surely reclaim our heart and learn again to call on this strength, this love, this authentic self.

Retrieving our Heart

Opening our closed heart is another way of describing the search for our abandoned selves. If we want to take our heart seriously and truly let go of our woulds, coulds and shoulds and projections that hide our true self, and if we want to live a more authentic life that is characterized by peace, clarity and depth, how do we do it? How do we act on the concept that we can undo our forgetting of our essential self and retrieve it so we can take our hearts to work?

Again, athletic or physical body examples may be helpful. The marathon runner as described in a previous chapter gets to mile 23 and feels helpless to continue.

In Yoga movement and postures, as described earlier, Participants are invited to hold a position or engage in a movement until it hurts so much we think we have to rest. If I can open my mind and my heart and believe I have it in me to continue for one more second, and then one more and then another, and if I keep observing the ache and breathe into the source of the ache and pain, a new energy arises and I can continue on in the position or movement with ease. I then feel a sense of wholeness, elation, expansiveness, peace and openness all throughout my body and my heart.

Riso and Hudson in their book the Wisdom of the Enneagram describe another method for cracking ourselves open to hear our Essence. They describe the art of "not knowing." Admitting we have forgotten who we are, what is important and not important, or how things ought to turn out, creates a quiet mind and can allow for a transformation of our state of mind and heart as well as that of others. Change and transformation cannot and do not occur without the heart being touched. We feel the call to our Essence in our hearts, and only our hearts can answer. What moves us is emotion, the movement of love. If our heart is closed, we will not be able to respond to the call of authenticity or open heartedness. **Wanting** to live from our heart is crucial for transformation. The marathon runner has a vision of the finish line, the artist sees his painting in his mind, the person wishing a more peaceful life envisions and desires it. The person with a tire seeping air, knows how a healthy tire looks. Knowing we want the peace and clarity and kindness of heart and admitting we do not know how to arrive at our vision, is the first step in achieving it.

Almaas describes not knowing as a form of emptiness. When we finally accept and feel our helplessness in the face of our anger or our fear or our loss of our heart, and when we experience it in a totally open and impartial manner, our tight emptiness loses its power and changes into a vast spaciousness. Not knowing involves giving up the conviction that we know what to do, and that we are inadequate because we cannot do it. Emptiness or not knowing, reveals to us its true nature, a deep and open inner peace. Experiencing this peace, is essential to exposing our hearts at work.

Aids to Retrieving Our Heart

Retrieving and listening to our heart is difficult and challenging work. It is difficult to do it alone. For myself, perhaps the increasing difficulty was a sign of my increased awareness of the importance of the work, that so many opportunities existed for change, as well as for support. I include here a few aids in doing the work. Some examples have been implemented in organizations to support leaders and staff in listening to and speaking from their hearts.

Circles of Trust®

Parker Palmer, in working with teachers in K-12 schools and with faculty members in community colleges, and with doctors, created the concept called Circles of Trust. A Circle Of Trust is a community of like-minded persons who use dialogue about a "great third thing" to prompt the ability to listen to one's own inner teacher (think heart). There is no fixing, no advice, no direct guidance, only the opportunity to explore one's personal truth as inspired by a poem or a story or a song. As we listen to the metaphor in a poem, for example, then listen to the truths of others, often our own heart opens and new insights occur to us and we are able to speak them to ourselves and to the circle. In this way our heart has been retrieved, we listen to it and we can be guided by it.

There are several benefits to the Circles of Trust, or being alone in community, because we need help to discern the heart's voice. One, the journey toward our heart is so challenging, we may get exhausted and feel like quitting. Second, the information we receive from our heart may be so subtle we don't discern it without dialogue. Third, we need company to help us be courageous enough to go where our heart may take us. For a greater understanding of Circles of Trust, I highly recommend reading Parker Palmer's book, *Hidden Wholeness: Journey Toward an Undivided Life.*

In community colleges all across the country, faculty and staff members are participating in Circles of Trust. Facilitators are trained by the Center for Renewal and Wholeness in Higher Education in the Dallas Community College District. K-12 teachers, doctors, leaders are trained by the Center for Courage and Renewal. Each of their organizations are experiencing, as a result, a sense of personal renewal that is transforming their following and their leading. Organizations are creating dialogue groups around significant topics of concern to all, faculty members are changing their approach to teaching and learning and staff members are building bridges of trust with all aspects of personnel, including students and patients and clients. Another Chapter in this book gives greater detail about how Circles of Trust function.

Journal Writing

Writing about our day, or our response to a poem, a story or an experience can be a significant way to call on and to listen to our heart. In retreat experiences where we have been invited to journal for a period of time, say 20 to 25 minutes, I have begun to think, "What else can I possibly say about this idea, why did the facilitator suggest writing for 25 minutes; it's way too long for this activity." Asking the question becomes the very act of "not knowing," and it allows a kind of emptiness and suddenly our heart can take over and we begin to write things we didn't know we felt or knew. As I write this chapter, I feel stumped about how to describe something. The minute I admit to not knowing, ideas come to me and I find myself saying things I didn't know I would. Novelists describe their experience with characters in their books who begin to direct their writing and create outcomes they didn't know would occur. The same can be said for journal writing. The experience of writing, especially writing about a recent or a past personal experience can be the tool for remembering who we are at our core and we suddenly realize our heart, has reappeared. I will always treasure the advice I once received to write in my journal with my left hand. I suddenly found myself writing advice to myself in the voice of a six year old child who remembered something I needed to remember as an adult. The act of not knowing and vulnerability created by writing with my left hand, opened my heart and I was flooded me with insight.

Physical Activities

Yoga classes focus on movement or on holding postures until the body is filled with the energy I described earlier on these pages. Once the body is filled with a new energy and the heart is open and the inner self feels open and spacious, we are invited to stop, strike a quiet pose and then simply LISTEN. During these times we may be inundated with the pure qualities of our heart: love, kindness, clarity, strength, joy, truth, peace, warmth, fulfillment, commitment, solidity, definiteness, confidence, groundedness, and certainty. The physical activity assists us to focus on "not knowing" and helps to promote a quiet mind and invites our heart to arise within us.

Other physical activities as in the marathon runner I described earlier, can assist us to reach into that space within us and call on our heart. One of my favorite movies is The Legend of Baggar Vance. In this story, a former golf pro is damaged emotionally by his experience as a soldier during WWI. His tragic loss of troops causes her to lose himself, his authentic self, and that includes his golf swing. Baggar Vance appears and begins to coach him—not just to find his swing but to find his true self wherein lies his swing. This excerpt in many ways is a brilliant summary of this chapter on finding heart.

The Legend of Bagger Vance

> Inside each and every one of us is
> One true authentic swing . . .
> Something that can't be taught to you or learned . . .
> It's something that's got to be remembered.
> Over time, the world can rob us of that swing.
> . . . You have to look with soft eyes.

The golf swing and hitting the ball become metaphors for finding our one, true-self; our heart. When we can put ourselves in the space of not thinking, (not knowing) of listening, of being physically one with everything and everyone around us, we are more likely to look at the world with soft eyes and to get out of the way of our heart and feel it re-emerge.

I've actually had this kind of experience on a golf course. I'm a beginning and very poor golfer, but I love being physically in the most beautiful spots in the world (surrounded by glorious mountains or the ocean or rolling hills). Sometimes when I stand at the tee, I feel a gentle breeze flow around me, I feel surrounded and filled by a presence, and a peace and an energy that is uncommon for me. When I am in this space, open and vulnerable and at peace I now believe I am in touch with my true self at those moments, and guess what? It makes a difference in my golf swing and my drive. The marathon runner experiences something similar. At the moment energy dwindles to zero, the runner feels it is impossible to continue. However, if she acknowledges this not knowing how she can possibly continue, and if she breathes into her heart and legs and keeps going, a renewed source of physical and psychological energy carries her to the finish line.

Grounding and Cleansing

When I left my presidency with very poor health, I moved to New York City. Although I was dismayed by having to seek a new doctor, I was amazed at the M.D. I discovered. The first time I met with him, I told him my symptoms that included endocrine deficiencies. He said to me very kindly, "What you have here is an energy problem." He said, "I have the same problem, I'm feeling really exhausted today and I've acquired this cough, let's work on it together." He proceeded to teach me to ground and cleanse my energy.

We sat together and looked at a space on the floor in front of us with our eyes open. He guided me to think of pulling my energy down and into my physical being and then cleansing my energy. I felt my feet on the floor. I felt my toes, my hands, my ears. Later he guided me to a series of seminars by Christine Schenk where I learned to think of energy as waves and layers and I began to cleanse using a non-visual organizing of those waves and layers. I also learned, after grounding and cleansing to LISTEN to my heart or as Schenk refers to my Energy Body. I realize the grounding and cleansing is yet another way to develop a quiet mind and a space of not knowing and retrieving my true heart.

Conclusion

Living an authentic life or living from our heart is important for ourselves and for our work place and for those we serve. Finding our hearts by using various approaches, is essential for us so that we can then bring our hearts to our workplace in a safe and grounded manner. Although we are born as authentic beings, we often lose ourselves and lose our way, and we need to find threads that can take us back to our authentic self, our heart. When we are not in touch with our heart we may feel anxious, fearful, angry, and/

or depressed. We start to play Chess with our organizations. When we are in touch with our heart we feel calm, peaceful, strong and loving.

Poetry, story telling, dialogue, journal writing, Yoga, and other physical activities all can be stimuli for retrieving our heart or calling on our true, authentic self. Insights for action may come at these times or not. Sometimes we simply find ourselves moving in a new direction and we later realize we have been guided by an energy that comes from a deep place at our core, not from our will. Sometimes we just feel loved and loving and open and spacious and we are able to move through our day with a sense of groundedness and peace. Sometimes we are in the middle of a conflict in a meeting or a personal relationship and we have a new insight into the Other. We see anew what is truly valuable and we see not with our mind but with our heart. This is what it is like to live the authentic life, to find our heart to live guided by our heart.

We can transform ourselves, our relationships, our clients, our employees, and our organizations. We can continue to cast our shadow self on those around us by living out of our ego or personality, or we can learn to retrieve, our HEART and bring greater job satisfaction, high morale, and creativity to our work and to our place of work. Then we will be able to co-create truly productive and inspired organizations.

A Soldier's Heart to Heart

by Brian Delate

"Out beyond ideas of wrongdoing and rightdoing, there is a

field.

I'll meet you there."—Rumi

When I was in the sixth grade our teacher showed us a detailed documentary concerning the human heart which I watched with amazement. I decided then and there I would become a heart surgeon and began to memorize all the factoids such as the heart beats about two and a half billion times in an average lifespan and pumps approximately one million barrels of blood during that time. I would draw pictures of the different components—vena cava (superior and inferior), the aorta, the four chambers, septum—and explain their functions to anyone who would listen. Yes, I would become a heart surgeon.

Unfortunately, I was hampered in this pursuit by a terrible reading problem. I was a very slow reader at best and my comprehension was dismal. If asked to read out loud, I would stutter and mispronounce words; the resulting classroom laughter was riotous and humiliating. I was also hampered by routine bouts of violence. If I was in a rage I didn't care how much bigger or smaller my adversaries were. I would fight ferociously but foolishly, so you could flip a coin as to the outcome.

My great escape, before, during and after that time was anything to do with war. When I was little, I played with toy soldiers and built models of the B-24 bombers my dad flew in World War II. In the working-class neighborhood of the eastern Pennsylvania town where we lived, the other boys and I would play soldiers—mostly WWII, since that was our fathers' war and they had won. And the movies! I watched anything from WWII, such as *Bataan*, *Back to Bataan*, *Wake Island*, and *Bridge on the River Kwai*.

In 1968, at the height of the Vietnam War, our country was becoming sharply divided. I had barely finished high school and forgotten about the idea of college and medical school. I was working in a record store, reveling in the music of Jim, Jimi and Janis, and since I was definitely not college material, I was about to be drafted into the army. I knew a few guys who were running off to Canada or getting into any college they could since that would provide a draft deferment. I wasn't eager to go to Vietnam, but I didn't seem to have much choice, and I didn't know anyone who could pull strings to get me into a National Guard unit.

Ever since I was a boy playing soldiers, I had wondered what it would be like to be tested as a man. Would I be a coward? Or would I be able to take it? I was about to find out, and this was only the rehearsal for the real thing that would follow. In August 1968, I was drafted into the army and took a train with a bunch of other guys from Philadelphia to Fort Bragg, North Carolina. As I entered basic training, I decided to give myself over to the situation.

I was away from home for the first time, so basic training was quite a shock, along with being grueling and challenging. Almost all of our Drill Sergeants were combat veterans, sometimes twice over, and I was curious what these men were like before the trauma of combat. A couple of them seemed so psychically wounded and heartless; I didn't understand why they were still in the service.

What surprised me was that as much as the Drill Sergeants could intimidate, bully and humiliate us, I responded in a powerful and skillful fashion. I discovered that I had leadership ability and remained a squad leader throughout the entire nine weeks—no easy feat, believe me. I was also a steady, crack shot and possessed an intuition and expertise with any weapon I touched. Except for one other guy in our company, I could low-crawl faster than anybody. I was in the best physical shape of my life.

I was on my way to Vietnam at age nineteen with only five months of training, and upon arrival as a FNG ("fuckin' new guy"), I was in awe of the more experienced and weathered-looking soldiers. They had already survived dancing with Mr. Death and they seemed strangely relaxed. Would I become like them? Would I get home in one piece? Would I even get home?

Two pivotal events occurred soon after my arrival in Vietnam. With well under a year in the army and about four months in-country, I was made a Sergeant. For awhile, my rank was inconsequential, but then I was placed in charge of experienced riflemen, conducting night-time perimeter patrols. Feeling tremendous purpose and responsibility, I made my men aware that I cared about them and that I was ever mindful of their safety. As I learned then and later, trust is a very sensitive issue for most soldiers and veterans, and one which must be earned.

The other thing was the first casualty I witnessed on my first night in Chu Lai. I will never forget the first dead American I saw—a very cool black guy from Philadelphia. We sat together at a movie outside and less than an hour later he was dead. During the rocket attack that night, reality slapped me with the knowledge that people were trying to kill me—nobody had ever tried to kill me before—and they would try to kill me many more times after that. I was taken into the deepest arenas of fear I would ever know in my life. In the first few months of my one year tour, I dodged many a mortar and rocket, was shot at, crash-landed in two helicopters and heard Mr. Death singing the Animals song, "We Got to Get out Of This Place." I was there maybe six months when I began to feel like some of the weathered guys I saw when I first arrived. And in answer to my own question about whether I would be a coward or could take it, I discovered I experienced both. I would be crapping my pants and somehow pull the trigger. *Was this courage?*

After more than eight months in Vietnam, I became mostly involved in night work. I felt fully entrenched and had gained a sixth sense as to where and when danger might strike. What I had lost in innocence, I gained in cynicism but my skin began to express my anxiety. I had ringworm, jungle rot and something else I couldn't pronounce. All of it was spreading from my groin to my face and the discomfort was driving me into violent mood swings. One morning after coming in from a night shift outside the wire, I looked derisively at a Vietnamese man, a particular kind of guy we called a Cowboy, who then spat at me.

The rest is like a dream—I pulled this guy off his motor-scooter and proceeded to methodically beat him until I couldn't pick up my arms. At times I was ten feet overhead watching the savagery with a numb wonder but he was tough and scrappy, and would not surrender. My guys sat down and lit cigarettes, saying, "He needs to get this out of his system." After a couple of minutes, with my arms and fists on empty, and with this guy still trying to spit at me, I delivered a single kick from my jungle boot. I saw his eye pop out of his head. Somewhere deep in my core, I thought I might be insane.

Since I was getting so little sleep because of my skin problems, the doctors and medics in Chu Lai decided I should go to the hospital in DaNang, where the only dermatologist in Vietnam was located. He would give me the right medicine so I could return to my unit. Maybe I would stay that night and drink before returning to Chu Lai.

It was overcast as I hitchhiked from where a Huey helicopter had dropped me off in the middle of the day on the outskirts of DaNang. I was picked up by an old man driving a severely rundown truck, with about a dozen little kids in it. I climbed into the cab of the truck with the old man and some of these children. Immediately the kids began to touch my shoulder, my hand and my jacket. They were playful and curious and tried to handle my .38 pistol, which was in a shoulder holster. There isn't any energy quite as alive and wondrous as that exuded by little boys and girls and it penetrated my fog. After we all settled in for the slow and bumpy ride, the old man told me he was from Germany, was a Catholic missionary and was one of many. *Wow, that's interesting.* Here he was, wearing a quiet sense of purpose in a war zone and looking after orphaned children. How could that be? Maybe he was a World War II veteran.

He dropped me off at an intersection and pointed out the street he thought would take me to the hospital. I walked a few blocks and realized I was lost. Now I had to be careful since it was not smart to be alone like this. For no particular reason, I walked up a set of stone steps that led to a simple garden and a small pond. "I'm going to sit and have a cigarette," I thought, and as I did, I looked at my dark mirror image in the pond and wondered, "Do I know who this guy is? What am I doing here in this part of the world? Will I ever see my girlfriend and family again? Why am I living in this life-and-death situation where it's always hot and everybody is losing their mind?"

As I tried to look more deeply into my reflection, I heard a door open. On the other side of the garden a Vietnamese man appeared. We looked at one another and instantly I felt my .38 under my shoulder. My attention disconnected from the pond and I suddenly became hyper vigilant of the man's actions. He was doing some chore that sent him back and forth across the garden.

I deduced from his appearance that he was a monk so I relaxed and lit up another Marlboro. Then I noticed the garden, where there were flowers with odd shapes and vibrant colors I had never seen before. They smelled sweet, almost hiding the decaying tropical odors of

DaNang. The monk and I exchanged neutral looks each time he crossed. After his third or fourth trip, I looked up and realized I was next to a pagoda. *Wow, this place is old, maybe hundreds of years old.*

Years later I would realize that I had been sitting in front of a meditation pool. The monk and I never spoke, but there was a communion between us and maybe a trust. Like the German missionary, he had a quiet sense of purpose. He was a Holy Man, but I really didn't know what that meant at the time. I wondered if he was being good now because he had been bad at some time in his past. Then he stopped crossing and I was alone again with my reflection. As I rose to leave, I thought about that Vietnamese Cowboy I had beaten so badly and now felt the weight of my actions.

As I tried to retrace my steps to where the old German missionary had dropped me off, I got lost even more. But now there were people gathering; mostly bigger kids who wanted to sell me something—their sisters, dope, anything. Behind these bigger kids, there were three Vietnamese Cowboys, like the one I had bloodied in Chu Lai. They weren't interested in selling me anything. They wanted whatever I had and didn't care how they got it—and I was by myself. *Oh man, maybe this is some kind of karmic payback.* I managed to scare the kids away, but not these guys. One of them kept asking me for a cigarette while another one was trying to get behind me. I felt like Humphrey Bogart at the end of *Treasure of the Sierra Madre* when the bandit leader barks, "I don't need no stinkin' badge!"

I finally took my pistol out and relaxed my stance, but I wasn't really relaxed at all. I had never shot anyone who was right in front of me. This wasn't like shooting into tree lines from a helicopter or from behind sandbags into the jungle. This was up close and truly personal. I was pissed and scared, really scared. I warned them, almost in a stage whisper, "Dung lai, motherfucker!" I cocked the hammer and thought, "Oh, my God, am I going to have to shoot these guys!?" A split second before I was about to open up on the one to my left, who was closest, the one in the middle backed off.

Then the others stepped back. Then I stepped back. It felt like I had eluded a pack of hyenas.

What was remarkable about that situation was that I did not shoot. I came so, so close. But I thought about the old German missionary and especially about the monk at the pagoda and my reflection in that pool and how I had been slowed down. It occurred to me that maybe there was a connection in bridging, possibly heart to heart, with the old German missionary and those orphans, and especially with that monk, and not killing those men. I would think about this for some time to come.

I found my way to a different intersection and got a ride from a couple of MP's in a jeep, who dropped me off at the hospital where I registered to see the dermatologist. I planned to get whatever medicine I needed and then hit an NCO club to throw back a few whiskeys. The doctor had me take off my fatigue jacket, took one look and then quickly admitted me. I started to argue, "You don't understand, Doctor, I have to go back to my unit!"

"No, you don't understand!" he shot back. "You're not going anywhere, Sarge."

I was immediately escorted to a bank of showers with a bunch of different medicines to apply to my skin and then put into a hospital gown. I found myself in the dermatology ward, which had no TV or music, and about fifteen other guys with every skin problem you could imagine. They gathered around me as I sat on my bed while brief introductions were made. Then they just stood there like they were waiting for something.

That something turned out to be a nurse, who brought in a large bottle of purple liquid medicine and some small sponges. She was tall, wore well-pressed jungle fatigues and no makeup. Her female energy was powerful in this setting, but she evidently reserved her charm for other circumstances. It was exciting to see an American woman but with all those guys there fantasy was impossible.

"I need you to remove your gown, Sergeant," she said, quietly and professionally.

"Really, you do?" I began to glow with embarrassment as the blood ran to my face and, thankfully, not to some other part.

She just nodded and the other guys laughed.

"Okay, you guys, back to your cages, now!" She was stern, but not mean.

I took my gown off and the nurse gently and professionally painted the afflicted parts of my body—my thighs, groin, buttocks, chest, neck and face—with the deep purple-reddish medicine which made me look like a bad version of those Scottish warriors in the movie *Braveheart*. There was no excitement to report and she would do this for me everyday.

Realizing I would be in the hospital for at least a week, I asked the nurse that first day if my parents would be told I was there.

"Oh, they'll get a letter."

That was alarming. "Really, what kind of letter?"

"That you're here for a while, that's all."

Jeez! My mom will think I lost my legs or something. I better write my own letter right away. I had been sugar-coating my experience in letters home since I'd arrived so I sat on my bed and quickly scribbled down, "Dear Mom and Dad, I'm in the hospital in DaNang. Nothing to worry about. I'm fine—just some skin problems. I'm okay, everything is okay. Really, I'm fine. I'll be back in my unit in about ten days."

Each morning a nervous and much too cheery chaplain's assistant would come to visit me and offer counsel or light conversation. "So, good morning . . . ah, Sergeant or ah . . . can I call you Brian?" His

34

body language said, "Oh God, this is repulsive—I hope I don't catch anything here." *What a fuckin' square . . .* I just rolled my eyes, stared at him and muttered something like, "Can you just move on?"

And he did. I remained cold and dismissive, but he kept coming back each day. On the third or fourth day, I found myself talking to this guy and we had a couple of light and sincere conversations about our families. I wish I'd had the wherewithal to apologize for my rude attitude when we first met, but I didn't at that time.

I left the hospital a little more than a week later and headed back to my unit in Chu Lai. I had gotten some real rest, and my skin was on the mend, although the purple stains from the medicine took a couple of months to fade. I felt like I'd been rescued from myself and, for a brief moment in time, I didn't feel like the soldier/warrior/sergeant. I felt relieved and even calm.

When I arrived back at my company, the mail clerk gave me a small stack of mail. There were letters from my girlfriend, my parents and one from my sister, who didn't write that much. Back then, the mail took anywhere from five to ten days each way, and her letter was dated about the time I entered the hospital.

It read, "Dear Brian, last night Mom came into my room and she was crying. She said she dreamt that you were standing at the end of the bed, saying she shouldn't worry and that you were okay, that you were all right. Are you?" *Whoa!* I told my buddies that was like right out of a Twilight Zone episode.

The serenity I had briefly experienced as a result of my hospital stay was soon overrun by the demands of the war. Our company was now dealing with increased racial strife. A couple of guys tried to kill our cold-hearted commanding officer and fortunately failed. Drugs were becoming a big problem and, oh yeah, we were still fighting the enemy who wanted to kill us. I won a decoration near the end of my tour doing extremely dangerous work, but I would not appreciate that medal for many years to come. By the time my year was up, I had stepped into a deeper madness of not caring whether I lived or died.

Still, one of the most difficult days I experienced in Vietnam was the day I left my company to go home. As my friends and I walked to the Jeep that would take me to the airstrip, I started to shake uncontrollably. *What the hell is this?* Then tears suddenly blinked out of my eyes. *Oh, my God, I don't want to leave! How could that be? I lived for this day.* But the very deep bonds of these friendships were being pulled apart and it really hurt. My buddies and I managed to laugh our way through it, shook hands and hugged it out a little. Then, zap, I was home, back in Pennsylvania, where it snowed the next day.

The year back home was a different kind of madness. I drank daily, scared my family, hurt my girlfriend, wrecked cars and didn't care about anything. I was on the verge of suicide or homicide with growing frequency. Luckily, I felt like I had nothing to lose and decided to try a couple of summer courses at the local community college. They were remedial, but one was an experimental class that addressed reading disabilities. *Maybe it's finally time to deal with that problem.* Well, that class worked and totally changed my life. I felt like Helen Keller, when her world opens up with that fascinating language using fingers and hands. I became an academic achiever and was even excelling in math—go figure. In the middle of my second semester I was doing so well I thought, "Maybe I'll become a pre-med major. Yeah, why not? Maybe, medical school . . . Sure, that's possible. A heart surgeon? That might be stretching it."

In my second year of college, I took an acting class because I couldn't get the math teacher I wanted. What turned me on was that acting was more than reading and words—acting was about how to live with words, how to behave with them and how to call on feelings from my life to give life to those words. It also tapped into some of the same fears I knew from the war, minus the bullets. I switched my major from pre-med and transferred to Rider University, where in 1975 I graduated with a degree in theatre.

I moved to New York City, and after spending some time adjusting to city life, began to have a career in acting. I'm fortunate to have had my share of good parts, and to have worked with very talented and creative men and women. I've had success in each arena—plays, film and television. I've worked in different cities around the country and have even gotten to do a hit play in London and shoot a film in Germany.

I was in New York on the morning of September 11, 2001 just after a successful summer stock experience in the Berkshires where I was actually playing a Vietnam veteran. I watched in amazement and horror as the first jet passed over my head and plowed into the north tower of the World Trade Center. By this time, prayer was a part of my life and my reaction in that moment was to pray for the souls that had just perished. As I walked to my apartment, I suddenly became furious with God and ripped at my shirt and cursed Her out loud. "Why did you make me witness that!? God damn it! God damn you!" Deep and invisible wounds had been opened—Vietnam was returning like a comet to the forefront of my consciousness.

Along with acting, I had begun to dabble in screenplay writing, cooking up a story that might make an interesting family drama in order to create a part for myself that I'd always wanted—romantic lead. But as I was being haunted in this new way from the war, I started writing down some of my experiences for a potential one-man show. Unexpectedly, some of the war experiences from the one-man show found their way into the screenplay I was writing.

But the writing came to a halt in the months that followed September 11, as I sank into a very deep despair. The war was alive in my life again. Maybe a month later, I was sitting in our living room when my wife and daughter came home. My young daughter's first remark was, "Daddy, you're sitting in the dark!?" I heard the heightened concern in my daughter's voice and snapped out of my morbid reflection. *Jesus Christ, I am sitting in the dark.* I put on a cheerful facade, "You're right honey, let's get some light on here."

I was sinking fast and decided to search for counseling and found it through the Veterans Administration and with fellow veterans. My curiosity went beyond myself and I found my heart-to-heart dialogue with other veterans had a healing effect. I didn't feel as alone and a special kind of restoration took place. Also, at this time I went into unknown territory with something called Energy Body Medicine taught by Christine Schenk who came to New York from Germany to give classes about chakras and centers, or as I would later refer to them, "invisible muscles." So, as when I went to college, I was stretching the envelope as I learned to delve deeper into the meaning of life.

All of these tools helped me to express my feelings and remembrances in a vehicle that was uniquely mine. What began to take shape for me, on paper at least, was the screenplay for the film I would actually make a couple years later entitled *Soldier's Heart*, referring to an expression from the Civil War for what we now call PTSD (Post Traumatic Stress Disorder). I prefer "Soldier's Heart"—it's more poetic. Because I had been cultivating a spiritual life, I now believed in transformation and I felt compelled to share some of my own transformation in this little independent feature film.

The making of *Soldier's Heart* was quite a struggle. Had it not been for another Vietnam veteran and key friends to help, I could not have made the film. As writer, director and producer—I even took a supporting role as an actor—I felt I was reliving the responsibilities I had known as a young sergeant. There was great risk, but this time nobody was trying to kill me. They say a samurai warrior is not given his sword until he has mastered an art form, and this movie was my art form.

Then I met Dr. Edward Tick, who has worked with restoring veterans for more than thirty years. I was given his book, *War and the Soul*, by a fellow veteran and was astonished by Dr. Tick's insights in regard to PTSD and the historical facts relating to Warrior/Soldier cultures. Dr. Tick's institute in Albany, NY is also called Soldier's Heart—a beautiful coincidence. After reading *War and the Soul* and participating in one of his PTSD workshops; I showed my film, *Soldier's Heart,* to one of his training groups which was mostly made up of health care professionals who were learning to treat PTSD and some veterans. I asked Dr. Tick if I could try an exercise with his group that was an echo from the film's story.

The main character of *Soldier's Heart*, Elliot, a Vietnam vet, begins to take responsibility for what is missing in his life, and decides to write a letter to himself from his now-deceased father (a World War II vet) who had never written a letter to Elliot the entire time he served in Vietnam. (This was something I experienced in my own life with my own father.) As a way to heal that hurt, Elliot writes the letter he would like to have received from his father at a time when he really needed it.

This exercise provides a subtle, but nonetheless powerful, catharsis and is one of many ways veterans can begin the process of restoration. The clinicians and veterans in that group sincerely responded to this exercise and one man, a non-veteran whose brother had been killed in Vietnam when he was eleven years old, wrote the letter he wished his brother could have written to him just before he died. Dr. Tick then had a veteran in the group read that letter back to this man. With true compassion, the rest of the group witnessed this remarkable piece of healing.

On another occasion, I screened the film for two Vietnam veterans in my editing room. One was a friend, and I did not know the other man. After the lights came up, it was silent. My friend nodded his approval of the film but the other man left without saying anything. The next day my friend called me to say that he had been quite moved because the film allowed him to reflect on his own experience as a marine, and that the other man had not been able to speak, because he had to go home and write a letter to his son who was serving in Iraq.

Recently we premiered the film at the G.I. Film Festival in Washington, D.C. where it won the Best Narrative Feature Award. The founders said that even though it's a quiet movie, we won because of the quality of the responses to the film, not the number of people who attended the screening. In a surprise moment at the festival, during a panel discussion with active duty military chaplains, I suddenly remembered my rudeness to that chaplain's assistant I had encountered in the hospital in Da Nang back in 1969. I raised my hand and as my heart raced, I shared that story because I wanted to acknowledge the significance of these men in front of me, as spiritual buffers between armed combatants and God, but also because I wanted to express my gratitude to that chaplain's assistant. He had been kind to me at a time when I was unaware of my desperate need for kindness. The chaplains smiled graciously and offered to bless my film, which they did.

One of my best friends in high school, who served in a recon unit in the Central Highlands and had a very tough tour in Vietnam the same year that I was there, came down from Baltimore to see the G.I. Film Festival screening. He hardly ever spoke about his combat experience, but his soldier's heart was touched that day.

Through his tears he said, "The day we landed in California from Vietnam, some demonstrators . . . they threw eggs at me." In that moment I was able to say to my friend, "Welcome Home," and we embraced heartily.

Afterwards, he felt embarrassed because of his tears. We went off to a corner of the lobby, and we had a conversation as intimate and powerful as two men could have. He thanked me for the film and I thanked him for coming and for sharing his emotions. I was now fulfilling a deeper purpose.

What a journey so far to go from the angry, learning-disabled kid with a fantastic ambition in the sixth grade of becoming a heart surgeon; and arriving at a place in life where my encounters as a soldier in war, a student, a professional actor, a Vietnam veteran and now a filmmaker would result in expressing myself as I do today. I have come to believe I am blessed, both as a veteran and as an artist, to have been able to bring my experience in life and war together and apply it to my craft. I feel I have been ultimately led by the heart and that in this way I have become a healer of the heart, the heart surgeon I once wanted to be.

Choreography of the Heart
by Jonathan Hollander

It is the supreme art of the teacher to awaken joy in creative

*expression and knowledge. *Albert Einstein**

"Our relationship with America will never be the same, since your visit to Cambodia." This remark from the King of Cambodia after Battery Dance Company's week-long residency in Phnom Penh epitomizes the impact of our work in the arena of international cultural engagement. The collaborative work we do to facilitate individual self-expression results in artistic excellence, social relevance and transformation in a way never achieved when I choreographed in a vacuum, creating every step of a dance piece by myself.

The Hearts of Students

Joyous Energies

Battery Dance Company has worked with New York City high school students for decades. We engage in cultural diplomacy, often in third-world environments, and we bring together local and international dance groups and people in the city for an annual outdoor Downtown Dance Festival. In addition, we produce an annual New York Season premiering our latest works. I am always looking for new ways to bring our mantra of artistic excellence and social relevance into play. An important step in my evolution as an artistic director and our development as a company occurred at Frank Sinatra School for the Arts in New York City. We created an experimental platform I call Joyous Energies, because that was the name of a new piece created by students at the school. It showed what high school students were capable of achieving if given the right kind of guidance and the opportunity. This experience became the foundation for the collaborative process we call Dancing to Connect.

The Frank Sinatra School of the Arts was open to experimentation, and one of my former dancers was on the faculty. This relationship created space for a synergy and organic building process. As an artist, I believe that all the arts—music, dance and the visual arts—are intertwined; and all are very important in whatever creative enterprise I tackle.The school has all those areas separated into different departments that operate independently. The students from one department don't interact with students in other departments and teachers don't work together to create projects that bring these themes together. We saw this as an opportunity to listen and share and experiment in a new way.

Over the course of the 2nd and 3rd year of our residency at the school, I brought in three well-known musicians with whom I had been working in my own creative projects with Battery Dance Company. They did a two-day intensive workshop with music students and I sat in for part of it. What I witnessed was students learning tools by which they could create their own music. They also worked with poetry, bringing in the literary side as well. Poetry was created by the students themselves to which were added poems by Herman Melville and Michael Ondaatje that the musicians brought to the table.

Art students listened to the music created by their peers and designed costumes and scenery that they felt would complement the score. Finally, in the reverse of the usual order of things, the dance students were introduced to the music and the visual designs and set about the task of creating movement that suited the music, scenery and costumes.

The net result was incredibly complex—totally unlike anything they had done during the course of their first two years. We had opened up a creative space in which young people could express themselves in word, sound, design and movement—we had given them a whole new voice. They were so proud, and they said to me, because I was the witness to their work, 'How do you like what we created? They owned it! Joyous Energies became a platform we could use as a guide to future work in American schools as well as overseas in our efforts as cultural diplomats.

The Blue House Project

About the same time, I became aware that an old friend, Dr. Christiane Walesch-Schneller, a was working on an inspiring project in Breisach, the small German town where she lived. The *Blue House* is a living memorial created by the community of Breisach to commemorate the Jewish families who had lived in peace with their Christian neighbors for 300 years until the Nazi times. Most of the Jews of Briesach perished in concentration camps, while the lucky few fled through circuitous routes to safety in the United States or Israel. My friend had turned over a big part of her life to this project, and her devotion and that of the large number of volunteers who participated in the project was very inspiring to me. It moved me that a non-Jewish person would care so much about what had happened before she was born, in a town she moved into when she married. Through the act of researching the history of the Breisacher Jewish community and sharing this information with the community and particularly the younger generations for whom the Holocaust was a chapter in a history book seemed to me to be a beautiful and touching act. I began to conceptualize a collaboration with my friend and the *Blue House* after I discovered that another New York City choreographer, Aviva Geismar, was the child of a survivor from Breisach. Aviva had had no knowledge of the details of her father's background, an illustration of the fact that in tragic circumstances such as the Holocaust, neither survivors nor perpetrators want their past exposed to their children. They want their children to live happily and without the painful history that they, themselves, can never forget.

Aviva and I went to Germany with funding from the US Embassy in Berlin. We visited the *Blue House* and met with concerned individuals and leaders in the community with whom we discussed our ideas of performing in Breisach in and around the *Blue* House and the nearby historic amphitheater. Eventually, what was originally envisioned as a performance-based project metamorphosed into an educational program, prompted by the question posed by the local community leaders: "Could you work with students?" As I think back on this moment, it seems a miracle that the suggestion came from the community and not from Aviva and me. That was transformational: the success of the project was therefore far more likely because the Germans had suggested it and therefore, took responsibility for enlisting the schools and convincing the education office of the City of Freiburg. We could incorporate what I'd learned at the Frank Sinatra School of the Arts, and integrate the thoughts and experiences of young people in Breisach into music and movement.

When we entered the German environment as Americans, the last thing we wanted to do was imply that we were there to teach and preach about the Holocaust. Instead, we explained that we were there because we were impressed with the honesty of the community in facing its history so courageously. As a result, the students were able to come to their own conclusions and to adopt their own stance.

Out of the five dances that were created that summer, there was a wide range of expression. Several of the pieces drew on the image of outsiders threatened by conformists. One piece, was especially poignant—the solo dancer who became an emblem of the outsider was a young woman, 15 years old who looked about 12 because she had a growth hormone deficiency. She was of Lebanese heritage, and, it later turned out, was terminally ill. I remember saying to her, when I was coaching her, "You need to think of something really, really, sad so that your face and body convey the right emotion." Like any teenager, she had displayed self-consciousness and inappropriate looks in her portrayal. Afterwards, I was looking through the beautiful images taken by Ari Nahor, the photographer who was documenting the process. When I commented on this particular girl, he told me about her condition and, I burst into tears. Nothing could have prepared us for the way in which the German students addressed deep emotions through choreography, an art form which was new to almost all of them. We discovered that that they hungered to deal with the subject of being an outcast. Students, in their teenage years face many transitions: they're angry with their parents, and they're angry with their society and all the turmoil. In this experience, their anger and frustration found a creative outlet, a place for expression.

Students interacted with events from history. Non-Jewish, German and immigrant students explored in an abstract. yet deeply emotional ways, the crisis of the terrible event in recent German history. They created their own way of expressing their feelings in gesture and movement, and in the end, danced their self expression The community response was overwhelming. The following quote is from the German newspaper, Die mt den Stühlen tanzen "Dancing for the Blue House" in Breisach. The theme was a difficult one: the deportation of the Jews from Breisach, to whom Aviva Geismar's Grandmother belonged. That dance could be a medium, through which the past could be re-enacted, no one could have imagined before this performance.

The almost heart wrenching and unrepeatable intensity of the Breisach Performance made the Freiburg one (the following year) a happy, exuberant and poetically easy performance. Five schools, six "Young Dance-Makers Creations": What one could imagine to result from six days of workshops working on this performance, was only a sliver of the performance the audience saw. As it is so often in dance, the movements stand alone, without a concrete meaning."

When I saw the results of this work, the transforming impact on students, the creative and artistic excellence of the dance movement, and the powerful audience response, it changed the way I looked at my art. I discovered that creating a safe space for people where they could explore their own experience and then express it openly, resulted in a power I could not create by myself. As a result, Dancing to Connect, is now a signature component of Battery Dance Company. We use it in our schools program, in all our cultural diplomacy, and now, I share the creative experience with my dancers.

The Hearts of Professional Dancers

The Old Way, An Environment of Fear

I have always considered myself a social person. From a very early age, I have liked people and liked being around and engaged with people. When I was very young in the dance world, I was around people like Merce Cunningham and Twyla Tharp who were masterful. I perceived them as being very, very self-contained and hermetic. It was really clear that my way would be different. I wanted to create a friendly environment for dancers. I wanted it to be a happy place. I didn't want it to be competitive, back-biting, dangerous.

I didn't succeed at first because I was too harsh and my pressure on myself, to succeed, caused me to make overly burdensome demands on my dancers, and I didn't always get the results I was looking for. It turned out that I had made a typical dance company with a director and the dancers and the dancers coming late; and the director (I) would scream at them. One or two dancers would always be problematic; they would always be late, and they would always forget the steps or re-arrange them. It was an impossible thing. I think it's partly about maturity. I wasn't confident enough. I didn't have the same ability to take risks as I do now. I was planning everything painstakingly and methodically and I think the impact of my work was diminished. It was really mine. It was what I could imagine. The hearts of my dancers were stifled.

I remember getting physically sick. I would get nauseous because I'd be in the studio dancing like I was taking a class, ballet class. I would do something over and over again, until I could figure out how it was done. Then I would sit down and notate the sequence on a legal pad. Then I would get up and start over again. It was a horrible process, and that's how I would create. I would create all this work, and then I would give it to the dancers, and I would criticize them until they got it right. It was painful for everyone. By and large, minus the legal pad, this is how the creative process worked in most dance companies, although some choreographers explored different approaches. From what I've seen and read, Mark

Morris creates in the studio with his dancers. Balanchine was known for doing that.

Twyla Tharp used to improvise—she would video tape herself improvising and her dancers would view the tape and figure out how to do it. She hated teaching it, and she couldn't remember what she had done. She was a brilliant mover, so it made sense to do it that way. As long as she had people around her who were amazing enough and committed enough to do that. And she did.

So, as a result of my experiences with the students at Frank Sinatra School and the students in Germany, and also with other artists like those I brought in to the Frank Sinatra School, I began to be more collaborative with the dancers in my company.

The New Way, Creating Space for Creative Voice

Since I've started creating with my dancers in the studio, I feel the work is much bigger and broader because it's the combined energy and spirit of more people. There's a lot of opening for dancers to develop their own material and to improvise and it happens in very little steps. It is a fluid, creative process with my dancers. Our new pieces and the new way of working are all consistent with my change with the loosening up of the control of the boundaries of who's the creator and who's the interpreter.

Preparing for Creativity

With every new creation, there's a substantial period, for me, of getting ready. With the piece, *Shell Games*, for example, I pulled together a lot of source material. The material had to do with the inner and outer self, role playing. How you present yourself outwardly and who you really are inside. I observed the elections and the debates leading up to them between John Kerry and George H. Bush. I observed those men answering questions or not answering them; I thought about their personas. The election of the new pope was also happening at the same time. I've spent a lot of time in Poland, and the Polish people are very Catholic and they were deeply engaged with the previous pope who was Polish. We began to see images of the new pope with Armani and Versace designed gear. He approached his window, they opened the window, and whoosh he's there, with an audience of tens of thousands of people and somehow his presence does something for them. He looks very snazzy in his new Armani raiments, but what's that all about? Why is he qualified to deliver higher order information and advice for people? Leadership and guidance, the president, the pope, that's what *Shell Games* is all about. It's about the dichotomy between the powerful and the powerless. The dancers in my studio know no power in life. They are disrespected by the public at large. We are considered a lower order by a lot of people. You're a dancer; oh, how cute. That dichotomy between the people who are respected and those who have no respect, all of that is my research that went into that piece.

How Collaboration Works at Battery Dance Company

The next step in collaboration is the art and the music. With *Shell Games*, at first, I thought I would collaborate with a visual artist who lives in this area. I went to his art exhibit and I went to his studio and I thought we might build something together. I met with Frank Carlberg, the musician, and we had some brainstorming sessions. Somehow all that didn't play out the way I thought it would. The artist ended up not having an active role, though Frank did. It was Sole Salvo, the costume designer, who ended up being my partner and who created amazing physical forms for this concept. Frank's music took off on its own. What we tend to do, Frank and I, is just talk and exchange what we care about and then he goes and creates unique, magnificent and unpredictable musical scores.

When I collaborate with choreography or musical composition, I find someone whose work I think is fabulous and who is in control of his/her process. I don't really get involved in what Frank is going to do. I try to approach it like you see the clouds. I see it. We talk about practical matters: how long it's going to be, will there be sections with breaks in between, how many instruments will we use, because we're already thinking about how we travel with the piece.

The key basically is the music. Frank created the score for *Shell Games* and his musicians built it. When he chose the lines by Brion Gysin, "I am that I am," and picked a Gertrude Stein Poem, Very fine is my valentine. It all seemed very incongruous. Audiences are sometimes put off by the repetitive lines "I am that I am" But no one has questioned the power of the piece—it's very effective. Frank is an imaginative person, and his act unlocks my act which unlocks the dancers' act.

Then the dancers get involved. I bring the music into the studio. We all listen to it. It's very spontaneous. I say, OK, I want to work with you two, and then I'll come back to others. I do that instead of working in unison, and I don't know why. It's just very intuitive. I am sort of charting the course. Then, as things go along, we build up a structure together. Someone might say, what about this? And we explore that possibility.

We usually start with improvisation. With *I'll Take You There*, the entire first two minutes were total improvisation without a single dance step. We set up a frame, and for the first rehearsals, movements were different every time the dancers did them. Then we locked it in. I knew there had to be something strongly contrasting to improvisation, and so I inserted precise dance movements. We whet the palette and then we go into something else. It's doing the same phrase with different movements. We all know the same vocabulary: there are turns, jumps, balance, kicks, adagio.

We can do it all, and we explore various combinations together. I may see someone practicing something in the studio, and I say, "Wow, that looks great, let's do that in our new piece." So they're contributing raw material as Louise Nevelson did with her sculptures; dancers bring in found objects, and we add them to the creation. This experience has had an impact on my relationship with the dancers in my company.

How Dancers Respond

In the beginning, I think I wasn't a very fun person in the studio. I wasn't good to be around. I was demanding and critical and harsh as I said before. I have changed and I've let go of exclusive control of the creative process and shared it with the dancers.

I think my dancers now really enjoy being around me. After working with me for three months and after having worked with another choreographer for several years, one dancer said, "I keep waiting for you to scream at me." I kept appreciating what she did, and she kept waiting for the other shoe to drop. I think a lot of dancers are used to abusive behavior. Another dancer told me about very abusive situations he had been through. He'd had opportunities, very lucrative opportunities come his way, and he's turned them down.

I have heard people from sources really far away and close at home say that my company has a unique feel to it. The dancers and others describe our culture as one of mutual respect and openness and courage. We have a reputation for being very humanistic and for being a fine environment to work in. That is wonderful, and I think that draws people to us. I think this also has an impact on those who witness our work, the audience.

Audience Impact

People have noticed the quality of the dancers; they're dancing at such a high level. I don't know if they'd be doing that if they were not happy with what they're doing. There is a noticeable difference between dancing technically well and moving with expressive beauty. In our last performances there was a new level of finesse. The dancers didn't have much time to engage with a new piece, and yet, the end product was moving and effective. One long-term board member said of our new piece, *I'll Take you There*, "This is the best piece Jonathan has ever done."

Conclusion

My 35 year career with Battery Dance Company has been a wonderful journey in self-discovery and in discovering the hidden resources of high school students, other artists and my dancers. The people with whom I have had the privilege to work have helped me to change and grow. This includes the dancers in my company who are ready for more. They're just so much more than a pawn for me to move around on the board. I have learned from Frank Carlberg, a most phenomenally talented and humble musician/ composer. I spent a lot of time with him; he created a large amount of music for me, and he was a really good peer and also a mentor. I respect his incredible intelligence and, his musical background, from Finland, which is of a very high order. Then I saw him in action and heard the music he created with his musicians. I realized that exciting and creative material was resulting from improvisation, despite the fact that he could have notated everything. That was a profound inspiration to me. He trusted his musicians, and he picked musicians who had wellsprings of creativity that can blend with one another; their creativity harmonizes.

I am now able to do that with my dancers, and I'm able to create a space, an environment of genuine respect and compassion, courage to take risks, and yes, love for one another and for our art. It makes a difference in our lives, and it makes a difference in our artistic excellence and our social relevance.

Creating for Children

By Ginna Gemmell

Introduction

The source of creativity is each individual's rich inner life, their heart. When heart is allowed to flourish and manifest in an organization, the products of the organization are interesting and unusual. The users, in the case of Fisher-Price toys, children, are the primary beneficiaries. The secondary beneficiaries are the employees themselves. This was one of my first lessons when I began to work for this unique and exciting toy manufacturer.

I was delivered to Fisher-Price toys straight from the Appalachian Regional Commission (ARC) in Washington, DC to the snowy Spring of East Aurora, NY. I was placed in a glass fronted office in the Research and Development (R & D) building, a ski chalet-style structure on the campus of the famous toy-maker. I landed into a busy dream-state that lasted five years.

My first memory of the place was of a Senior Designer who strolled down the hallway in front of my office and said to his colleague.

"Oh look, Fisher-Price (F-P) has a new doll and they've put her in a window box." I wondered, "Have these guys ever worked with a professional woman before?." I later learned that I was the Company's first female manager in any department other than Human Resources (HR) and, therefore, became an instant novelty. This feeling of endangered species changed for me as the '80's progressed and more women were offered leadership roles at F-P and elsewhere in Corporate America. With it changed the toys, formerly geared to boys, which soon expanded to include those designed specifically to meet girls' interests, as well. I decided to approach my position gently and not overwhelm the design and engineering team with my vision for them, which came to me during my first few weeks and would unduly frighten them because of the changes that would be required. Rather I seeded ideas until everyone thought they had been incubating for several seasons. The ideas met a receptive audience in the many freshly minted designers who were hired at about the same time.

I grew in power over time, first through the power of my position as market information bearer and then through personal power. In six months, my Director called me into his office for my first review. With it came a 40% raise in salary. I must have looked astonished because Paul assured me that while I was doing a good job, the large increase came because the VP of HR, had discovered that I was doing the same work as my Marketing male counterpart and this was to redress the inequality. I was very grateful to MaryAnn and realized that I had the benefit of silent top cover.

I spent my initial weeks reviewing earlier prototype toy research studies as a strategy for more fully understanding the scope of my new job as Manager of New Product Research. Anxious and eager, I was deep in study one afternoon when a little remote controlled car screamed into my office, circled my desk and left without signs of a human driver.

The little car broke the ice, making me laugh for the first time since arriving. I realized I had come to a special place where people actually played for a living.

Creating for children requires a community in dialogue

This was a dramatic change for me after my work at ARC as a policy analyst for child health and development issues around the Region, dealing with intractable economic and social issues. "I have really come to the North Pole and I'm working with Santa's elves and toys," I thought to myself. When I shared this observation with my new director, he seemed slightly offended. "We are serious craftsmen, Ginna, and toy making is a lot harder than you think—you'll see." I later observed how spot on that comment was; how everything we made seemed to be a miniature version of the adult world, crafted to scale to give a child power over it while insuring safe and economical use of the product. An early illustration of this underlying precept was found in our tape recorder and camera. It was important that we design everything as though it was destined for the adult world, only better and with play value. I learned that play value grew from actual play!

Conversations that Co-Create

A few weeks into my first year with Fisher-Price, as if to prove my colleague's testimony, three men staged a lively yet playful debate immediately outside my door for over 50 minutes. Their energetic conversation made it impossible not to eavesdrop. They launched into spirited dialogue about what should be the desired arc of the water spray squirting from the spout of a toy whale, a component of the new Fisher-Price bathtub set. They were very spontaneously yet very seriously, discussing the myriad aspects of the whale's squirting abilities in the context of enhancing play value while minimizing the splash effect on the bathroom floor. It was at that moment that I knew I had come to a truly amazing place. I subsequently learned two of these mischievous men were engineers and the third was a designer. Their playful, colorful and outrageous conversations occurred regularly in unusual places. Their hallway exchange was actually an informal problem solving meeting where each shared a diverse professional opinion of how to improve the smallest detail on one of many new toys in development. They were just doing their job, I learned. "Excellent, if not obsessive craftsmen," I thought to myself, "I have really come to a strange new world." I realized none of my other colleagues found it odd for engineers and designers to be spending this kind of time on details. These serious and careful people opened dialogue whenever and wherever the right people with the right information happened to be in the same hallway. Play was serious business!

Later, in the cafeteria, while everyone else mingled, chatting with one another, (R & D, Marketing, Engineering and Sales having leisurely conversational lunch), I immersed myself in The Washington Post fretting over Reagan's tax cuts and its impact on children's health and education, and the welfare of the people of Appalachia. Alarmed by the potential folly of Reagan's misguided action, I tried to politically engage my table companions. Everyone stopped talking and eating and looked at me. After a prolonged silence, one of them said (with great patience to a novice), "We vote, and we put the best people we can in Washington to represent us. Thereafter, we leave it to them to do a good job. Our job is to make the best toys in the world." I was stunned into silence and silently put the paper away. Slowly, they cured me of my severe case of *Potomac Fever* and the life I had left. They drew me into another realm where the distinct working style was very different from the one I left behind.

On days when the weather was pleasant everyone disappeared from their offices at 4:00 PM. Moments later, we assembled in the back yard of the R & D building where we played a friendly game of Bocce Ball while chatting informally about our projects. Management and designers *played* together, a practice that was encouraged. Later, as I learned more about creativity I realized this was an excursion. An excursion was a way to momentarily get distance from a problem, plug into the child in us, gain new perspective, and build relationships and share ideas. A side benefit I soon discovered was that it also served as a way to stay in shape and get some fresh air. These opportunities for relaxed conversation were one aspect of the environment leadership encouraged that supported connection with one another, listening to one another and seeing one another as real persons.

Traditions That Connect

The place was full of traditions. Perhaps a week prior to the Thanksgiving holiday a large, fresh turkey was delivered to my office one afternoon. In fact, I soon discovered everyone had received a turkey that day. Apparently, this tradition was started by Herman Fisher and Henry Price, who founded the Company in the 1930's. I believe this practice is in place to this day. I thought it was quaint but very caring and, ultimately, delicious!

Holidays and special occasions presented opportunities to share and celebrate. Halloween was an especially festive event at F-P that gave the excuse to stage parties where everyone tried to outdo the other, appearing in the most elaborate and creative costumes. One designer came as the four seasons while another transformed herself into a love seat. Not to be outdone, the engineers went wild with costume-bejeweled lights and sound effects, wearing creations that looked like trucks, *Husky Helpers* and space ships. We received gold coins at Christmastime and had big family picnics in the summer. These were happy days lived in an environment that fostered a sense of safety and support for the individual. It spawned creativity and ultimately new products for children.

Evaluation and the Creative Process

As I rode up the learning curve of my new world, I learned that 60 pairs of hands touched each toy before it went to market, and it took two years from the first sketch and initial research to get the toy to market.

Each and every one of the 50 new toys launched annually gestated through an accelerating gauntlet of evaluation meetings held every other month, every month, then every other week. New information flowed from the nursery, the field, and engineering, as well as domestic and international marketing and sales about the toy's veracity. Product selection meetings were held around a huge board room table in the R & D conference room, and anyone who had a stake in the product wedged themselves into the room.

In its initial concept stage, each designer was asked questions about the *idea* with the intention of developing it further. Historical precedents were cited and competitive products were both described and compared. In the next round its positioning was explored; What is it? What are its features and benefits? How does it work? How much does it cost to make, to market, to advertise? Those concepts sturdy enough to survive the scrutiny, morphed through a concept description to rendering a clay model, to a production model, to packaging and two levels of market research and then, toy store buyers before they finally received the Fisher-Price Brand name. When a prototype became available, it was not uncommon for us to play with it at the conference table and make suggestions. I learned that a lawn mower and tricycle popped up every few years and they weren't approved until they had been assessed for 10 years, when everything was just right. We never gave up.

My role was to present the early stage market research conducted with mothers. This developed into an art form because I wanted to treat every new concept developmentally, that is, focusing on ways to improve it and make it better. Sometimes, ideas were not destined to fly and I had to say that, too, like the Kermit the Frog outfit. Children loved Kermit but none of them wanted to be Kermit!

While hundreds of concepts passed through the committee every year, only 50 were selected.

Creative ideas flowed in the hallways and the cafeteria, as well as in our home living rooms around East Aurora, in formal Ideation Sessions and informal office chats and at dinner with friends. We conducted Exploratory Focus group Sessions with mothers to uncover unmet needs. Behind the one way mirrored glass wall, the gallery would be crammed with designers listening for clues. I traveled to many cities to conduct this research, and I often accompanied the design team to a local museum between group sessions for the inspiration art provided our ever-probing minds. After each Focus group we brought all of the designers into the room and conducted another mini-Focus group, often sketching out ideas right on the spot that would meet a need or a desire gleaned from mothers.

Sometimes an idea came out of sheer pain. I remember the evolution of the Fisher-Price Infant Monitor. Its genesis was in the tragic SIDS death of an infant who was the child of our HR Director. Everyone was deeply saddened by the event. Shortly thereafter, two designers and I were sitting in my office wondering aloud what could be done to prevent SIDS. A few days later, a rendering of the monitoring system we envisioned in our conversation emerged from Vic and Dave, director of Crib and Playpen. They immediately made our concept visual. We scheduled focus groups with new mothers to review the concept and get their input on how it might appeal to them. The focus group moderator shared the rendering and described its features.

With an audible, collective gasp the new mothers reacted, followed by a long silence. We knew we had struck a nerve and, while it represented a totally new product concept for us, it was immediately evident we were working on something very important.

We listened to the Mother's wishes for portability and convenience, and integrated their ideas into the forthcoming prototype. It took months to fine-tune, test and retest the monitor and write copy that did not promise the product as a safeguard against a SIDS death but, rather, only that Mothers could hear their infants from any room in the house. Presenting this to the Product Selection Committee was a challenge because it was not on Plan. Not only was the product new for F-P, but new to the world. We showed tapes of the new mothers reacting to the monitor to share their incredible certainty. There were technical problems with the monitor in getting a radio frequency that wouldn't interfere with other appliances in the home. We used gentle persuasion to work it through the product selection committee and tapped into their concern about avoiding SIDS, about helping anxious mothers while constantly working on the technical challenges. Only 200,000 were produced the first year, to manage the risk. Within the first month they sold out.

The monitor gave us the courage to press forward to create a whole new product category with many more "Parent Helpers" for Fisher-Price and the world. In moments of self-doubt or identity crisis consumers would always reassure us we were going in the right direction and that strength, safety, durability and good design were the hallmarks defining who we were. This was a seismic shift for the toy maker, resulting in more than doubling its revenue. How did the culture handle the success of a million units selling year-after-year? Staff held inherent values of humility, awe, understatement and an unflagging dedication to mothers and children. They never lost their moral compass.

Everyone continued to amaze me! How was it that they were so creative, so humble and so committed to kids all of the time? Were they for real? The statue of children that stands at the entrance to the Company's East Aurora, NY headquarters bears the inscription *"Our Work Is Child's Play."* It was true. Herman Fisher gave the Company guiding principles for every product: it must be colorful, it must make noise, it must have play value, it must be safe, it must be durable and it must be affordable. They didn't say that it needed to last 50 years, be over-engineered, loved by both children & mothers, or survive a fall from the top of a building to see if it would break. From my experience listening to Mothers I learned that F-P toys enjoyed a lively after market, too, through garage sales or stored for the next generation. This caring about children seemed to be part of their genetic code. They were so obsessive that the Consumer Product Safety Commission replicated their standards for the rest of the industry.

Growing Creative Culture

Once, during a visit to a new market research facility in nearby Buffalo, their staff said "You must be from Fisher-Price." While I had been with Fisher-Price for a year by then I was curious what made them think that. They said "You all sound alike and you're all just so nice, but you are all into the details." This puzzled and worried me. Why in the world would we all be alike? The perception that outsiders regarded us as similar remained with me and, the longer I stayed with them, the more I observed it.

The culture gave permission to speak the truth, discouraged criticism of others and encouraged collaboration. We shared the same town, the same reverence for children and the same obsession for creativity, quality and continuous improvement, and we looked for the same characteristics in new employees. I became obsessively creative about the research, constantly devising new approaches despite my team and me accomplishing hundreds of studies each year. I became known as the *"Gemmell Machine"* and, in short order, found myself producing at the pace of my colleagues. I had become just like them! I loved them, too. I was a little older than most of the young designers and treated them as younger siblings, but with total respect for their skills and vision.

How does all of this relate to creativity and authenticity? No one talked about being creative or authentic as a value. They manifested creativity in their thinking, and authenticity and honesty in their conversations and work together. It was expected and it was practiced by everyone in every position. Like a fractal, each department mirrored the same values and practices within their professional discipline. You could have taken a handful of diverse professionals into a room and found that they were very much like the ones you had just seen somewhere else around the organization.

We did have conflicts. I once went to my boss to complain about a marketing colleague and he said he would talk with her. Later, he came back and informed me the offender would do better the next time and would I please just focus on my work? Office politics were seen as a big waste of time. No matter what was going on in the world, we were focused on making the best toys in the world. There was no mandate to accept these values and put them into practice, they were simply the way they were. These were not rhetorical values. These were actual, living, breathing values. You had to observe, reflect and model them to fully understand what was desirable and worked well. If I erred, it was by imposing my well honed political skills in an environment that did not have use for them. I soon learned that respecting outstanding employees, not lobbying and quid pro quo, was the legal tender at Fisher-Price.

Hiring the Right People

F-P hired good, caring, talented people. We certainly hired slowly, insisting that every serious candidate be met by at least 20 people over the course of a two-day interview schedule. There was no room to hide in these interviews because we wore them out and their true characters appeared.

The early 80's were a fantastic time to assemble a team at Fisher-Price. Baby Boomers were starting their families so demographics were in our favor along with new technologies. Looking back in time, we were able to assemble probably the highest performing team in my career. Bobby was on-board before I arrived, about middle-aged and knew the history of the company very well. She was able to put it all into perspective for us and keep us grounded with her expertise in in-home testing. Walt and Nancy were freshly minted market researchers with incredible quantitative skills and techniques, giving us the ability to analyze trends and help develop complex products never before imagined at the Company; like a real working camera for toddlers. Nancy invented qualitative "Exploratory" research methods for infants that opened whole new worlds. It was a small, nimble team of four who related well to each other, the designers and the marketing department. We encouraged honest feedback, although were tender with each other's feelings. There was competition to do our best work, but not competition with one another and it was a very level playing field in decision making with a clear understanding of roles and responsibilities and clientship. We still keep in touch on "LinkedIn" after 25 years!

HR systems reinforced creativity and authenticity through this hiring process, through training, reviews, rewards and promotions. When a person had been in a position for 2-3 years they were offered a new role so they would constantly find challenge in learning something new and have the opportunity of viewing the Company from another perspective. Bored people couldn't make exceptional toys. Promotions usually came from within as staff members were carefully groomed to take more responsibility in the business. Collaboration was rewarded along with individual performance but there were no stars or designer signatures on the products.

Professional Development

Senior Designers mentored young designers and were held up as models. An MBA program was brought directly to our corporate campus affording convenience and access to managers and professionals who wished to round out their engineering or design educations with a business degree. F-P reimbursed every employee achieving an "A" 100% of their tuition course work, 75% for a "B," and 50% for a "C." The drive for academic excellence was rewarded. Within such a supportive environment no one was left hanging out on a limb. A flat management structure enabled access across the corporate spectrum to anyone you cared to approach. Everyone had their own office and because of the glass door entries, it was easy to determine if someone was available or busy. All the same, we sometimes needed an infusion of new ideas.

Occasionally, we found ourselves 'painted into a corner'. Having created or produced every toy possible, how could we possibly devise something new? When this happened we piled everyone on an airplane and headed for Synectics, in Cambridge, Mass. There, using the Synectics Creative Thinking Process, we generated hundreds of new ideas to fill our funnel.

At Synectics, we found a resource that augmented and enhanced our own creative culture. We learned the handles, "I wish" and "How to" to protect ideas and develop them further. We gave ideas headlines, and emphasized listening and paraphrasing skills to really understand one another. We explored developmental evaluation of an idea to make it more viable, creating a long list of plusses and framing our concerns with a "how to." This kept the dialogue, even about strange and unusual ideas, positive and safe; it invited further ideas to improve a concept.

Fisher Price was so supportive of the strategies we learned at Synectics, I eventually became a certified Synectics facilitator and integrated all their techniques into our on-going processes. We applied them to a myriad of R & D and marketing opportunities, as well as to problems in operations. We even modified Synectics' creative thinking techniques with linguistic exercises to create new product names and brought the process into focus groups where Mothers and kids could invent along with us. The process was a natural fit for the culture of F-P. On our own initiative, the Synectics process became integrated into our daily work. We discovered that creativity came from a source deep within ourselves that required self reflection, openness, vulnerability to one another and listening to our own place deep within ourselves as well as to one another. We learned that creativity comes from observing the world around us, staying open minded and the ability to make connections between unrelated things and being willing to offer beginning ideas that others can build upon. We also learned that all our freedom, conversation, play and debate worked best when our talk came from that still place at our individual core. Leaders at F-P had long held these values and made them visible to us in many ways.

Much later, when I left Fisher Price Toys, I was hired by Synectics as a full time consultant. When I worked with a new corporation, I would facilitate corporate meetings designed to create and develop new products and strategies. Emotions in these sessions ran to the euphoric with people reporting that they never had been so productive in working together, or felt so appreciated. I learned, though, I was essentially creating for them a "temporary culture" they could not sustain. Participants too often lamented this positive collaboration didn't last when they returned to their punishing home culture. Bringing Synectics creative strategies to a corporation tended to work better in cultures holding similar values of safe dialogue about new ideas and protection and appreciation of employee vulnerability. So, in some cases the process flourished, in others it floundered.

The process was completely lost in competitive and "make no mistake cultures" whose meetings looked like staged melodramas, where the hero often "died." I learned that creating a safe place for sharing ideas (from the heart, if you will) and for being appreciated was crucial rather than generating fear of failure or of looking inadequate. Generating and maintaining a creative and authentic culture in an organization is a discipline that everyone needs to model and foster from the very founder and the leadership to every level of an organization. Not every company was like Fisher-Price!

Individual Integrity and Creativity

Leaders modeled the values of the organization. Stories of the Founder and past Designers became lore. We learned these stories like heroic tales from Mythology, passing them on to new hires in the best of oral story telling tradition. I remember the day the desk of Fisher-Price founder, Herman Fisher, was moved into my Office. It was huge. To entrust it to my use was a curious honor. Near magical properties were attributed to the desk and sometimes Designers would place new prototypes on the corner to see if the desk would give a "sign" portending the future of their new concepts. Understanding that reflection and playfulness is at the core of creativity, we made time for such nonsense. On reflection, it seems the stories from the past became a benchmark for present work. We felt honor bound to be as good as or better than those who had preceded us. They felt like family, too, revered ancestors who had left us a wonderful legacy. Started during the Great Depression, this Company had always been successful applying the rules of the craftsman. That legacy would not be compromised on our watch. This tradition of craftsmanship was part of East Aurora's past as it was a community founded by the Arts and Crafts Roycroft furniture makers.

Workaholics need not apply as family and private lives were highly valued. I was admonished for working until six o'clock by Chuck, our Vice President of R & D, who said he did not want me to work long hours. "Just 8:00 AM 5:00 PM," he said. "That is enough time to do your job and if it isn't, we'll get you more help." This was true for everyone except, perhaps, the Designers who typically preferred working in the Model Room alone at night to meet a deadline. On another occasion Chuck reminded me that I was almost 35, and if my husband and I wanted to have a baby, we should go for it; that F-P would support me. He said that people with children had a deeper understanding of play and becoming a parent would give me new understanding. While in today's corporate culture such conversation would be regarded as politically incorrect, at the time I accepted it as intended. His intent was to develop me as a human, his spirit was one of absolute kindness. Fisher-Price did not try to supplant the family by asserting a larger-than-life sense of importance but, rather, endeavored to be a supporter of families.

During my tenure Fisher-Price was owned by Quaker Oats who shared many of the same values. It was an exceptional acquisition that did not compromise the F-P culture. They recognized that we were the toy experts and left us to figure out our own path. They did improve our forecasting process to help overcome the boom and bust cycle of the industry.

They also brought more sophisticated management practices such as the PMP (Performance Management Planning) process, and the 360 degree program to evaluate managers. They transferred a few of their own staff into various roles from time to time. I once had lunch with Quaker's CEO and found her very inquisitive, supportive and remarkably candid. It was a great fit. Even though I was given the opportunity to move to headquarters in Chicago, I was too engrossed by the actual toy makers to leave them.

If someone fell from grace, as in having developed a problem with alcohol, they were sent to a rehab facility and only permitted to return on a consulting basis following treatment. Because "they had lost credibility and respect," they were no longer allowed to lead. This only happened following months of coaching and thoughtful deliberation. Leadership was not to be taken for granted and, while a fallen leader was cared for, they were removed from office. In those very rare cases everyone knew what had happened, why it had happened and were sympathetic with the person. Nonetheless, all were in agreement with the decision. If reclaimed, that person went on to become a valued consultant or holder of the history and was never maligned. Often, tales about such individuals went like this: "He could accomplish more before his three martini lunch than most designers could in a full day." Or, "You know Herm Fisher always kept a bottle in his bottom drawer." So, even one of the founders was an offender, yet he was respected for his legacy and sought out for advice despite his problems.

Occasionally, business mistakes occurred. Some originated out of a desire to push a pet idea while others may have met our guiding principles but didn't meet market needs in some way or fit our brand identity. Like a basketball player who is charged with a foul they raised their hand and lowered their head in admitting to the offense. In the Fisher-Price corporate culture the offender was never fired or punished, just expected to do better, learn, change and keep on working. In response to a mistake I made I was supportively instructed, "Just don't do that again." The important thing was to learn from the mistake and incorporate the lesson. These lessons often made it into the F-P 'mythology' without revealing the individual identities of the mistake-maker. This enriched the organizational intelligence and learning with a body of knowledge available for new hires. This also supported risk-taking and acknowledged the inevitability of mistakes and failures in the creative process.

Toys, once launched, were very rarely recalled. However, when a flaw was discovered it was the Company that found out first. Immediately, the public would be informed and a procedure supporting product recall and consumer refund or replacement was implemented. This was a rare exception because In-Home research, Nursery research and quality control usually identified problems long before the toy was marketed.

Repeatedly, focus groups would tell us that consumers trusted F-P. We did everything in our individual and collective power to meet or exceed consumer expectations. Everyone was committed to delight children and do no harm. During my tenure I never knew anyone who didn't share and fully embrace those values in their work ethic. This may seem like an exaggeration but I never witnessed an exception to this impression. That simple focus point and vision kept us all on a narrow path.

During my tenure at F-P, toys were made in the US in plants strategically located in close proximity to the campus enabling us to easily communicate. The plants reflected the culture like a hologram. When I visited the floor where products were assembled, I observed that workers on the line seemed just as committed to the values as the rest of us. Most of these workers were mothers whose personal interests and commitment to children and safety reinforced an ethic that sought to prevent anything slipping by that was not up to standards of excellence. Their respected position and unique point of view prompted them to openly offer ideas for new products and improvements which were often taken.

Later, the toy manufacturing process moved off-shore. Designers and engineers traveled internationally to monitor manufacturing and transport the Fisher-Price way of doing business. Standards were maintained through the rigorous attention and personal sacrifice demanded of staff supporting this process through long, exhausting trips into distant cultures. However, this made the work more challenging.

The Washington Post reported that Fisher-Price recalled a category of toys made in China that were not up to Fisher-Price standards. Characteristically, they caught the mistake, admitted the shortcoming and they recalled over a million toys. This was a major blow and I can imagine the angst they must have felt. Nevertheless, this action demonstrated their continued adherence to F-P's internal code of honor; absorbing the financial pain while emerging with new learning of how to do it better the next time while preserving faith in a world that now reaches far beyond their nourishing community of excellence. They know the brand must keep the trust with Mothers to continue to flourish.

Toys of Integrity

The dark times are our truest test of character and there were dark times mostly initiated by factors outside of our control. Recessions and escalating oil prices always triggered a downturn in sales because the costs of raw material and transportation presented pressuring price points. The price of gasoline at the pumps claimed the discretionary income of young parents.

Periodically, hard times would drag on for months requiring belt-tightening and cost reduction. When these conditions prevailed we would ask: Can we make a new play set from an old mold? Does this product need to last for 50 years? Is every feature critical to the play value? These questions generate hard choices for the heart and soul of the craftsman.

Technological innovations, too, came along that were much more affordable. When the Electronic Music Unit (E.M.U.) replaced the more expensive Swiss music box mechanism it was very tough to accept. Those same Engineers who debated outside my Office about the whale were now asking me if I could tell the difference between "Teddy Bear's Picnic" when played by the music box compared with the E.M.U.? We could all tell the difference but had to make painful choices to keep the toys affordable. The upside to the E.M.U. technology was that it enabled us to make other fun sounds, like the sizzle effect on the play grill.

I recall a Senior Sales and Marketing VP, who was down in the dumps due to slumping sales. He asked me why I was smiling as I passed through R & D hallways. I replied I was smiling because I was glad to see him and very excited about what we were working on for two years down the road. Hearing this didn't improve his dour look, and so I suggested to him the alternative was to act discouraged and that designers, engineers and researchers couldn't make toys if they were depressed. He pondered that comment and agreed. His action was to hold onto his pain and shelter R & D from the reality of the 'street' for the next year.

Sales and marketing was right to protect toy makers. Keeping an eye on the future, confidence the economy would improve, trusting our legacy and responsibility to Mothers and children pulled us through. That creative drive supported our breakthrough into the world of juvenile furnishings and parent helpers. Somehow, we came out the other end of the tunnel stronger because we never stopped working, wondering, experimenting and innovating through the darkness. We encouraged one another and didn't fall into the "ain't it awful" trap. The organization protected us.

Five years into my life at F-P, my husband moved to an appointment with Boston University. It was also time for me to go. I had helped F-P through a major innovation from a toy company to a truly research-based product creator, and my work felt complete. I accepted a consulting position at Synectics, and I began to help a wide variety of organizations think their way into new opportunities and to work through creative problems. I left Fisher-Price but Fisher-Price never left me. Although R & D arranged a sensational going away party and presented me with a modified Mandy doll dressed in a replica of one of my outfits with a miniature prototype trunk accessory identical to the one I carried on countless research trips, a few months later, I was back working for Fisher-Price!

F-P staff called and asked if I would visit Spinnaker Software, also in Cambridge, who had a licensing relationship to create a new line of Fisher-Price Educational Software. I set up a lab study with children and computers in R & D and was very familiar with the software available for kids at the time. "You can help them understand the Fisher-Price 'look and feel,'" they said. Eighteen months later I was still at Spinnaker working to bring the F-P culture to a wild technology start-up. This was only partly successful, but I did make inroads in improving the design and quality by managing the group, the test lab and customer service. We also began testing product with teachers, parents and kids. I shouldn't have expected to transplant the F-P culture to Spinnaker. After all, they had their own high tech publishing culture, but shared the core value of respect for kids and a natural affinity for innovation which made them pioneers.

Conclusion

What did I take with me from Fisher-Price? I learned that regardless of whatever I put my hand to I should do it well. I learned to play, the importance of play and child-like abandon in finding my authentic voice. I learned to assume value in other's ideas and to deeply respect people who could make things with their hands. I learned that living values is more important than discussing them. I learned that in time of trouble it is best to stay focused on the positive potential and to keep working. I learned I don't work for the money; I work for the joy of accomplishing something new that has the potential of being remarkable for the consumer, the beneficiary of my work. I learned that creativity and innovation grow from reflection and from a source deep within me and others, and it can be modeled, taught, cultivated and nourished by like minded people and by an organizational culture. I learned that living with integrity and commitment to quality is smart over a long lifetime and for future generations. I learned that openness at work and the freedom of play creates a better experience for children and the toys, and ultimately for parents. I hope Fisher-Price staff sometimes tell stories of my time with them. I still connect when I see a child play with an F-P toy and love telling its mother a story about Fisher-Price and the long, playful dialogue that is the history of that toy.

Heart Centered Medicine
by Bill Manahan M.D.

The Heart of Medicine

The heart of medicine is listening to and being connected with a patient; it is every physician asking, "Who is this patient as a human being?" I think of the heart of medicine as coming from love, compassion, forgiveness; the virtues we think of when we think of our humanness. The traditional medical model comes more from our brain where we think of the virtues such as skills, information and technology. These are important also, but we don't think of them as heart centered; they are more related to the senses; we can see them, feel them, touch them. We live in a non-heart centered, dominator culture that is hierarchical. That culture has led us to a lot of tremendous discoveries and skills, and it's led led us to a disconnection from an awareness of our own bodies and from our hearts. I think the trick of most of life is to connect the yin and the yang, using our brain and also using our heart.

Heart is intuitive; it is about feelings. A heart centered physician listens to patients, really listens, to their concerns and the important elements about their lifestyle that may be having an impact on how they feel. Heart centered medicine takes time, and it involves being a good listener.

What allopathic medicine does best is take care of acute problems that are caused by an event or thing (such as a germ). Examples are broken bones, strokes, heart attacks, bad infections, surgical procedures, anesthesia and acute pain control, and acute allergic reactions. The heart of medicine is not nearly as important in those types of problems because we have explicit and wonderful therapies to take care of them. The patient does not really have to participate much in their recovery. It is with all the chronic problems such as arthritis, hypertension, asthma, intestinal problems, and osteoporosis that it is so important to involve the heart of the physician and the heart of the patient.

Forces that Shaped Me as a Physician

When I think about heart centered medicine in the work-place, I suspect not that many people are connected to their hearts at home. It's not just necessarily that they don't take a heart centered approach to work. Rather, I think that most of us don't know how to be in our heart in our lives. We're living in a culture where, whether we're at home, in the school or in the neighborhood, life is more head than heart related. I don't think we're very balanced. So I think this book, *Heart at Work*, is timely and very important.

I grew up in Madelia, Minnesota, in a family that was pretty functional. I had parents who were educated and professional people. My father was an attorney, my mother published the local newspaper, the Madelia Times Messenger, and I learned from them how to get along with people. In addition, Madelia is a small rural town that really fosters connections and heart relationships. People would help their neighbor with an oil change, and then feel OK about borrowing their lawnmower. The central telephone operator in the 1940's would give you a wake-up call if you called her late at night and asked her for it. People came over to 'borrow' a cup of sugar, and you would never really expect them to pay you back, although when you ran out of milk for your morning coffee, you felt perfectly free to run next door and 'borrow' it. Especially important, if "the little birdie" who lived in your neighborhood, saw you doing things you should not be doing, you'd better high-tail-it home and tell on yourself before that "birdie" did, because things worked out a lot better that way. As I look back, I see what a blessing that was for me. For some people living in a small town is difficult because they may be ostracized or picked on where in a larger town they may find their own tribe. So, a small town may not be good for everyone, but for me it was wonderful.

Right after medical school, I did my internship and then my wife, Diane, who was a nurse, and I went into the Peace Corps for three years. We spent two years in Malaysia and one year in Ghana, West Africa. That experience where doctors and nurses are in extremely short supply, disease is rampant, and the health needs are overwhelming, also shaped me. I worked in an aboriginal hospital in Malaysia and in public health in Ghana, and I expanded my world view from my small hometown of Madelia. My experience added to my belief that western medicine did not have a lot of the answers regarding what made people sick and what could make them well. One event that stretched my idea of what is possible with our bodies was watching Indian men walk across hot coals and not burn or injure their feet. I asked myself, "What is it about our minds and our spirits that can prevent burns on our bodies when walking on hot coals?" Witnessing those kinds of events that we "know are not possible" helped me realize that perhaps my patients and I could be empowered to heal ourselves without medications. This experience opened my mind and my heart to see how our heart and mind, body and spirit are interconnected. I found I needed to learn a lot more about what makes people ill and what can make them well. Working with patients in third world countries changed how I wanted to connect with patients, it influenced my concern for those who are underserved, and it fine-tuned my commitment to social justice.

Another major force that helped to bring more heart in my life and into my medical practice, was who I married. Diane Jansen was my high school sweetheart. She was beautiful and smart and fun and the more that people knew her, the more they loved her. She was a soul mate for me, and I thought I really knew how to relate to her after several years of marriage. However, she was quite a few lifetimes ahead of me in terms of evolving herself as a person. She helped me a great deal to work on myself, and to become who I am; she helped me to learn to listen and to communicate. I grew up in the 1940's and 50's and it was a struggle for me, a male, to learn to listen and to be truly present with another in conversation.

In 1968 in Kuala Lumpur while in the Peace Corps, we lived on a street in which our neighbors were Indian, Malay, and Chinese. Their religions were Hindu, Muslim and Buddhist while Diane and I were Catholic at that time. These individuals were all incredibly welcoming to us, though Malaysia is a country of Malay, Indians and Chinese. I had learned, as a Catholic, that only Catholics could go to heaven when they died. I recall that we were taught that not even other Christians would go much less Muslims, Buddhists or Hindus. The Catholic Church was adamant that anyone who was not a Catholic would not see God when they died. This whole year I'm thinking, this is not right; this is crazy, these are good people and they will definitely see God when they die. Then, just about that time, in 1968 or 1969, the Pope delivered his encyclical about the birth control pill. The pill had been available during the 1960's, and it had begun to be used even by Catholics. I was working in an aboriginal hospital where there was a great need for birth control. I'd been using it occasionally to help my patients, because, for one thing, it helped to reduce the maternal death rate. After mulling over these issues for some time, I decided I was ready to talk to Diane about being Catholic.

I came home from work one day, and I announced, "Diane, I'm not going to be a Catholic any more." Her face blanched, but she managed to maintain her usual calm manner, she said cooly, "Well, tell me about that." I was stunned by her drained complexion, but I persisted, "Well, this whole year, I've been thinking about two things. One, about our neighbors and the fact that the Catholic Church does not consider them being good enough to see God when they die because they're not Catholic. And, now a final coup d'tat is the Pope's Encyclical about birth control. Diane, we've been using birth control for five years, are you ready to stop using it? I can't stand the hypocrisy of it." Seeming unpeturbed by the audacity of the Catholic Church and the Pope, she countered, "How long have you been thinking about this?" I said, "Well, this whole last year." She mused a while then said very slowly, "You've been thinking about his for a full year, and you never brought it up or mentioned it to me." I said, "Well no, I hadn't decided yet." She said, "What do you mean, you hadn't decided yet?" I said, "Well, I just hadn't decided." Surely she understood that it is important for a man to get all his ideas clear and finalized before he brings them up to his wife for discussion.

For the next month we engaged in quite a discussion, because Diane kept saying, "Well, Bill, that's what relationships are all about. You talk about things where you are undecided or are questioning." The idea made me slightly numb. I remember having a feeling when she was talking to me, that what she was saying *must* be right. However, I had absolutely no experience in my life where I saw men talking to women regarding topics about which they were undecided. My construction boss didn't talk with his boss or the other workers about what he was going to do next. A football coach didn't talk with players about what he was going to do. Then there was my Dad. I was not aware of him speaking to my mother about anything when he was unsure. It was a time when a man would just come home and say, "Well, dear, we're gonna move to New York in two weeks," and she would say, "OK!" There wouldn't be a discussion about should there be this job change. My whole grounding and world view and training were about making decisions like a man.

So here I was engaging in this dialogue with myself about a pretty dangerous thing. I'm going to leave religion, and Diane had actually left the Lutheran religion and became a Catholic to marry me. I had moved ahead and made this decision without sharing my process with her. That was the full start of my growth as a person and as a physician, and a dramatic shift in my relationship with my wife. It was the beginning of caring, the beginning of being intimate in conversation and expressing feelings. It all made sense to me, but I didn't know how to do it. Diane taught me how to do it.

One of the first opportunities I had to implement my new listening skills and my new openness to people's stories was in my first medical practice in Mankato, Minnesota. In the early 1970's a mother came into my office and asked me if sugar had anything to do with her child being hyperactive and not sleeping. If you had asked nine out of ten doctors at that time if this was so, they would have said that studies did not show any correlation between sugar and behavior. I myself had done some reading and did not find any studies showing a relationship. However, I decided to listen to this mother instead of saying something negative, and I said to her, "Tell me more." She described her child after her birthday party having had ice cream, cake and candy. She said the child was very wired and acted differently from her normal behavior. She also said she had done some reading that suggested perhaps there was a connection. "Really, what are you reading?" I asked her. She mentioned Prevention Magazine and a book by a pediatrician, Ben Feingold, MD. I went to the hospital library and asked the librarian to collect information on sugar and hyperactivity. She came up with an armful of articles and books, all from European sources, including Dr. Feingold's book, Why Is Your Child Hyperactive. He believed that artificial colors, flavors, and sugars could cause hyperactivity (now known as ADHD) in children. I read all that literature, and it caused me to begin to make some big changes in my medical practice. Case reports, studies and experiences I read about opened my heart and my mind, my world view enlarged again, and this was primarily because I had learned to really listen to my patients with an open heart. This kind of listening is even more helpful to doctors today, because so many patients explore their symptoms on the internet, and a lot of what they learn is significant information. So listening and being open minded are truly important characteristics for medical doctors; we can learn from our patients.

The two biggest things I learned from Diane that affected my medical practice, were learning to share and learning to listen. Debra Tannen wrote a book, *You Just Don't Understand: Men and Women in Conversation.* She says that men have conversations shoulder to shoulder and women have conversations face to face. Women basically raised children and men went to war and went hunting. We, as men are more goal oriented. A lot of time that means telling someone what to do. As a physician and as a man, we're trained to give opinions and to fix problems. So when someone says they had a really bad day today at work, my natural response is "How can I fix that?" When, in fact, you may just want to share; you don't want my answers, you want empathy and heart. So what I learned was to have more of a face to face rather than a shoulder to shoulder conversations.

Learning to have a shared conversation took a long time, and the most important part of conversation that I learned was not the talking part, it was learning to listen. I also learned that communication often improved naturally when I aligned my desires and attitudes with my commitment to Diane, my honesty, and loving actions toward her. Putting my heart in the right place was as important as making my communication clear and timely.

My lessons learned from Diane and from my experiences in the Peace Corps helped me to learn how to listen to patients, to hear their story, and that was vital in my integrative practice. A very common experience for patients is to go to a doctor and feel they are not heard. We know now that being heard is an important part of the healing process, and the more I listened, the more I learned that could be helpful to patients. So much of what we experience with chronic, repetitive disease relates to our lifestyle, and so often it's not just about exercise and stress, it's anything in our life. It was vital to me that I learn to be a better listener in order to listen to the whole person and to be a better physician.

Traditional Western Medicine

The whole traditional medical system is based on a parent/child model. By that I mean, if you think of it in transactional terms, the parent is someone who tells the child what to do. The parent/child model is very much a brain-oriented model and not very heart related.We're trained as parents to keep kids from running in the street or grabbing them when they're in the street, or picking them up when they're injured in the street. We usually don't share stories with children about kids on bikes who fall, or talk with children about what might happen to them, or we don't have children make up stories about what might happen to kids who play in the street. This might be a more healthy approach, but it all takes time. So we hang onto the parent/child model of directing our children to "Stay Off the Street! and "If you don't I will grab you and I will punish you."

The medical model is the same parent/child model. The traditional medical model, views the physician as responsible for diagnosing an illness, deciding on an appropriate treatment, and assuring that that treatment is carried out as prescribed or we label the patient as non-compliant. That model actually works ok for emergencies and acute illnesses. For chronic disease, it does not work very well. We say, "Quit your bad eating and change your lifestyle, and if you don't, I'll give you a statin drug or a sinus drug, or a blood pressure drug, because I know you're not going to change your lifestyle anyway." Perhaps you've seen that cartoon of parents with a rope around their kids, and they're walking down the street? Doctors put a rope around you, reel you in, and give you drugs.

This model begins in pre-med, medical school and residency; there is a hierarchy and everything is top-down—we learn to give more importance to what we are thinking than to what we are feeling. When we go to a clinic, or to a hospital, we are faced with a lot of people in nursing and medicine, and the healing arts, who were in the beginning, usually very heart centered, and they thought that practicing medicine would be heart centered work. Then, their training and the system often brought them more into their head than their heart. So the patient, is viewed as passive, accepting, compliant, and dependent on the physician's medical knowledge and goodwill. In this environment, it's very hard for a physician to stay heart centered. So going to a clinic is like going to talk to a controlling parent—or it's like walking into a typical American business establishment.

In the 1960's and 70's medical practice managed to remain relatively heart centered. Originally, training may have been rather harsh and hierarchical, but then we went out into practices where one or two or three physicians were in their own office. The small physician's practice compared to a large clinic is somewhat similar to going into Best Buy versus a small electronic store run by one person or a husband and wife team selling you products. Or it's the difference between a large corporate auto repair garage versus going to the small, one person business where you know the person, you trust him, you never bother to get an estimate, you don't worry that he's going to do anything to your car that you don't need. When we left medical school, many of us would be in small practices, and we had the same patients for years. It was easy to be heart centered, because you knew your patients and you trusted them, and they knew you and trusted you.

Somewhere in the 1970's and definitely in the 80's we started making medicine a business. I remember talking about it with groups. Medicine was going to change; we were bringing in business managers, hospitals started buying up clinics, we started having certain coding rules, and we had to make sure we coded correctly, we monitored the length of patient visits because time was money, the coding made sure we got reimbursed by insurance and we were paid a certain way. We definitely increased income, but it decreased the heart centeredness and the connectedness we had with our patients.

It is true that sometimes the small practitioner does a lousy job, and sometimes the large organization has better quality control. The Mayo Clinic, for example, has a great deal of quality control over their doctors, and in general they do a wonderful job. At the same time, the Mayo Clinic is where you go for consultation, you don't necessarily go there for your routine care. When Mayo got into buying up small practices, it sometimes put restrictions on physicians because Mayo is a big business. It was difficult for integrative doctors to be part of that system.

I began to realize the way I felt about the rules and regulations of big clinics was similar to the way I had felt about religious doctrine. There are a lot of rules we are supposed to follow, but where is the heart and soul of what we think spirituality/medicine is? After reading a book by the Dalai Lama, I realized that even some religious leaders thought religion was not right for everyone, nor, I decided, was working in a well-run, large clinic. I left the Catholic Church and I left the big business of health care. I realized that I didn't do well in big organizations; I didn't do well with big church doctrine or or big clinic rules. I did better in my own private practice in Mankato than I did in the Mankato Clinic. The Mankato Clinic took great care of the bookkeeping and insurance and other administrative activities. However, in big clinics like that, the physicians make decisions that I felt were sometimes not very heart centered decisions. For example, they may decide to give a bigger bonus to the doctors and pay the receptionists less. That was not compatible with the way in which I thought the clinic should be managed. I would pay the receptionists more and pay the doctors also. It's just who I am.

For those physicians who are more heart oriented, going to work in the large medical system is entering a foreign culture. It's difficult to be heart centered in a culture that worries more about production and time than taking the time to listen to patients.

Even in medical school, I was an outlier. I was always questioning, "Why are all these people having all these problems," and I was always swimming up-stream trying to figure it out. Swimming upstream meant going against forces that set the parameters for medical choice. Those parameters included perceptions, positions and policies. Swimming upstream was hard work, because I was always challenging pre-conceived notions of traditional western medicine. For example, if three sisters came in with migraine headaches, it wouldn't make sense to me that all three would be treated the same. Yet western medicine is still very likely to do just that. You rule out other diseases, and then there is an appropriate protocol of what medications to use. If you have high cholesterol, the doctor says, "Oh your body has high cholesterol and I now need to fix you (like fixing a machine), and I'll put something in the machine to bring the cholesterol down. Oh and by the way, you should exercise more and have less stress." And that's about the amount of energy western medicine physicians spend on a majority of chronic illnesses.

If you and your four siblings came in to a traditional clinic with high cholesterol, we would very likely do the same thing for all of you. We rule out this and we rule out that, and we put you on the same dose of the same medicine. To me, even in medical school, that didn't make any sense. People are very different individuals and each is biochemically unique. It turns out a statin drug like Lipitor may really be magic for one of the four siblings. For two of you it won't do a thing, and for one of you it's going to have a bad side effect like skeletal muscle loss, diabetes or memory loss. So that's a problem with western medicine. We stereotype everyone as a diagnosis, and we forget the individual. So right from the beginning, it didn't make sense to me. I got interested in trying to figure it out: what was causing illness?

Integrative/Holistic (Heart Centered) Medicine

I approach medicine differently from traditional western medicine. I believe our bodies are infinitely wise, and they frequently are doing us a favor by having a problem. I also wish to promote a new paradigm for chronic disease care, health promotion, and disease prevention in which the physician's role is that of mentor, advisor, and coach rather than one of complete parental control and responsibility. The patient/physician relationship for people with a chronic illness begins with a discussion of the unique role and responsibilities that patients have in the treatment of their own illness.

Let me give an example. Consider that I have had four sinus infections this year, maybe I'm living in a basement with a rug that's moldy. It would really be good, to figure that out. Or, I'm living in a house where two people are smoking and I'm really reacting to second hand smoke. Or milk is a mucus former for me, and I'd better quit having my milk, ice cream and cheese every day." Those are simple things I would take the time to identify with people, and they might not have any more sinus infections. These kinds of things happen over and over again, and western medicine has not been very interested in swimming upstream to find out, "What is your body trying to tell you?" Medical school does little to really pursue that concept. The medical schools would be irritated at me for saying that, but that's why I say they give lip service to it. When you go to your medical doctor they give lip service to the fact that you should be exercising and quitting your smoking.

Having heart in medicine is really connecting with you; who are you as a human being? My relationship to my patient should be characterized by compassion, concern, and a genuine desire on my part to be truly helpful. What are the things in your life that caused your body, in its wisdom, to give you high cholesterol or high blood pressure? You're going to say "Genetics, my dad, my uncle." I say, "That's true, but there's a lot of things we can do to change the power of genetics." You may have to work at it a little harder than I do, but through stress reduction, dietary change, following your heart, doing what you like doing, eating in a certain way, I can markedly decrease your chances that you are going to have high blood pressure or high cholesterol, and I'm going to work with you to help you get there." At least two different studies by Ornish and Brown et al, and Esselstyn show that lifestyle changes can prevent and reverse heart disease. Instead we prescribe a statin drug, when probably out of five people, one of them should have a statin drug and four of them would not need one, if we spent just a fraction of the time, energy and money helping the individual sort out other factors causing cholesterol problems.

A common illness is asthma. Very often, I would see someone in my clinic with asthma and maybe a sinus infection for a first visit. They would come to me with a runny and stuffy nose and a feeling of fullness in the cheeks that would not go away, and the person was miserable. They might beg me for relief, and I would say, "I'll treat this right now, but if you want to be my patient, here's an eight page form to fill out, and I need you to come back for an hour and a half interview, to find out why you, a 38 year old, non smoking woman, are being bothered so much by asthma and sinus infection."

Most people, especially a large majority of women and about 50% of men, would be very happy to be fully evaluated. They'd say, "For five years I've been going to doctors and they just give me medicine and I've been wondering what might be the cause of my problems."

So, a few weeks later, I would see this person in my office once again, but now for a thorough evaluation and visit. Her symptoms would have been relieved, and she would have filled out the form, and then I would spend an hour or more taking a history of her whole life; I would simply sit and listen while asking a few questions. At the end of the interview, I'd do a physical exam looking for little signs of allergies like difficulty breathing, rashes or itching skin or chest congestion. I would check fingernails for signs of zinc deficiency, but most of the time, the things we look for in an exam like that are fairly minimal. Then, I might say, our time is up, but come back next week, and we'll spend a half hour going over the information we sorted though through in this visit.

In the next visit, for a half hour, I would say, "Here is what you told me last week." I would have a list of seven to ten things in her life that were possibly affecting her asthma or sinuses or his migraine headaches or his irritable bowel, his high blood pressure or high cholesterol or whatever illness different individuals faced. So for the woman with asthma, I might say. "What I understand is that you haven't changed the rug in your bedroom for 15 years. About nine years ago, you had a water spill in on that rug, so you probably have some mold in there. I would recommend tearing up that whole rug. Secondly you haven't changed the mattress on your bed for about 12 years, it still feels fine, but it's full of dust mites. You haven't changed your pillows for seven years. You're using a big blanket all winter long that your rarely clean." So I talk about how much time is spent in each room and just look at the physical impacts of those issues in a house.

Then I look at other habits. "In the morning you wake up, you don't eat breakfast, and you have a sweet roll and have a cup of coffee. You know, there are a number of studies (including Ringsdorf, Sanchez and Kijak et al) that show how sugar is an immune system depressant. So you get a little infection and that turns into your sinus infection and that flares up your asthma. You're going to need to look at your diet, because you are eating way too much sugar, which is an immune system depressant. This means it weakens the immune system, allowing repeated infections and other health problems to occur more easily. We all get viruses, the question is, why do yours go into an infection that bothers you? You're a 38 year old, healthy, non-smoking female. You should just barely feel the effect of your exposure. The fact that you're a teacher and you're exposed to kids, you're exposed to even more viruses. Yet, you should go through the year without having an infection that puts you in bed. Third, you're involved with three volunteer organizations, you have two children, even though you have a very supportive husband, you've been under a lot of stress. Stress also weakens your immune system. If you are willing to address these issues over the next six months, I believe there is good reason to suspect that your asthma and sinus infections will stop."

A majority of people are willing to make the changes and they change their life. They say, "Oh my God, I have the power to make myself healthy!" In the current system, we feel helpless. If we have high blood pressure, we feel helpless; we need a physician to fix us. The truth is, we mostly need to make adjustments in our lifestyle. A two week change in diet can sometimes change a person's migraine headaches or their high blood pressure rather remarkably.

These and many other health issues are ones I have been privileged to address over the course of my career in medicine. Creating a private practice, a wellness center, an open door health center for the underserved and underinsured, and teaching and consulting in the field of integrative medicine, have nourished my life and, I believe, have enriched and provided some possible models for the field of heart centered medicine.

Heart Centered Medicine in Practice

Original Medical Practice

In my original practice in Mankato, Minnesota in the 1970's and 1980's, I practiced alone in the beginning, along with a receptionist, a nurse and lab person. All of them were fabulous human beings, we got along well, every day was a delight to go to work, and patients loved coming to the clinic. It was everyone's ideal of being in a medical practice. Soon I got a partner, just out of residency; he was great addition, and we hired one more employee to work with him. We didn't need a lot of meetings or conscious collaboration. We had just the right people in place, and there was a sense of equality. We each had our role in patient care and we were clear about each of our roles. We may have had a formal meeting every now and then, but lot of times we ate our bag lunch together or we'd go next door to Wally's Wagon Wheel Cafe, and we met informally over lunch. It was just easy.

We all had the same beliefs about holistic medicine, and the entire clinic was established around the principles in which we believed: we spent time with patients, patients became the heart of our practice, and we listened to them, we taught people how to listen to their bodies and empowered them to improve their own health.

Wellness Center of Minnesota

In 1982, Chuck Lofy and I started the Wellness Center of Minnesota. The purpose of that Center was to bring more holistic care to people and to work with businesses in the Mankato area to help them start wellness programs. We had a broad range of alternatives to western medicine that we offered to patients to assist them with shifting their lifestyle. A Naturopathic physician came one day each week, an exercise physiologist, a dietitian and a spiritual counselor, a nurse practitioner who was an addiction specialist, and two other counselors were on staff. We based our center in a renovated Catholic High School, Good Counsel Academy on the hill in Mankato. We also offered weekend workshops and seminars and for over-night events, people could stay right at Good Counsel. It was one of the first integrative centers in the United States. The entire staff met every Wednesday noon and we'd share cases; I learned so much from each practitioner. All I knew then, in the early 80's, was allopathic medicine. So I'm grateful that early in my medical career, I could learn from all these different practitioners. At lunch, as people shared their cases, each practitioner, reflecting their diverse perspective, would say, "Did you think of this?" or "Did you ask about this?" I'd say to myself, "Wow, I thought I was really a good doctor, and I missed basic stuff."

I felt so good when my partner, Chuck, and I started the Center, and it was sad when we had to close it. Chuck and I were the right people with the right idea at the wrong time. Today there are many integrative wellness centers in the Twin Cities, and there is a good one right in Mankato also. If I started that same clinic with the same staff now in Edina or Eden Prairie, MN, I believe that it would be successful. We had such an incredible group of people there. When I look back, I just say to myself, "We were in Mankato in 1982. Mankato is a relatively conservative community in Southern Minnesota. People felt insurance should pay for every medical service, but insurance companies were not willing to work with us, and so people had to pay for their medical care themselves without the assistance of insurance. One problem that still remains throughout the U.S. is that heart centered doctors who do traditional western medicine and large scale holistic medicine, have to drop insurance, because, in a sense, insurance dropped them. Insurers don't pay for a lot of what we do, because a lot of what we do is time related. We have a wonderful system for acute care, but that takes care of only a third of patients. My experience is that two thirds of the medical system is broken and lost, the part of the system that focuses on chronic disease.

In the last five to ten years people's attitudes about paying for holistic services have changed. People realize, if they're going to get a massage or acupuncture, they're going to pay for it. But any service provided by a practitioner in my clinic, patients felt that insurance should pay for it. People wouldn't pay $500 for eight biofeedback treatments, even if I assured that person they would have a good chance of eliminating their migraine headaches or decreasing their blood pressure. We had a fabulous biofeedback therapist.

In retrospect, I realize the Center was a good template for future centers, it was a great experience for us; we loved each other, we loved working together. When people in the late 80's would say, "How's the Wellness Center of Minnesota doing?" I'd ask, "Do you mean emotionally, socially, mentally, or do you mean financially?" Because emotionally, socially and mentally, we loved it. It was, every day, a great place to work.

We never had the benefit of a benefactor at the Wellness Center. Chuck and I had the stability and the name recognition at that time, to go to the people in Mankato and ask ten people for $10,000 to make the Center go. But we were not the kind of people to do that; it was our weakness in regard to money. We didn't care about money, and we didn't pay ourselves. Chuck was teaching at Mankato State University, and I had my private medical practice. So that's how we could make it economically. We lost a lot of money in our weekend classes because we'd do a whole weekend class with 8 to 12 participants and we were charging as little as $100.00. Education is expensive; it takes so much time.

The good part of being able to see the future, and create something like a Wellness Center in the early 1980's, is that it's an exciting life. The bad part is you tend to be 20 to 40 years ahead of what society is willing to pay for. You can see so clearly what's going to happen to the future of healthcare, and so it's painful when it doesn't work in the present. We ended up saying, "Why isn't this working?" It wasn't going to work in Mankato at that time unless we got a benefactor, and it's not who we were to ask others for money. In retrospect, that was a mistake we made in not being more business oriented.

Open Door Health Center

In 1990 after operating the Wellness Center for eight or nine years, I morphed the Center into the Open Door Health Center: a clinic for the underserved and the uninsured. After twenty years, that clinic is still successful. Most of the Wellness Center staff left, and we changed our focus from integrative medicine to giving very basic medical, dental and social services to people who can't afford to get basic health services. I brought in a Homeopath and a Chiropractor, but mainly, we just tried to take care of the medical needs of the underserved and uninsured. I am really excited because Open Door just received a $2.5 million dollar federal grant to provide basic, core services. There are eight dental chairs, two dentists, and two practitioners seeing patients along with social services and other services offered.

It was a blessing the Wellness Center turned into an Open Door Center for the underserved and noninsured. In addition to holistic medicine, one of the other loves of my life is poverty medicine and treating the underserved. Things happen for a reason, and the Open Door Center is a great service now for people in Southern Minnesota.

Education for Holistic Medicine

From 1997 to 2002, I worked on staff Center for Spirituality and Healing at the University of Minnesota. During this time, I administered the Open Door Health Center two days a week, and I worked at the University three days a week. The center was created by my cousin, Mary Jo Kreitzer. Mary Jo was a nurse practitioner in my private practice in the 1970's, and together we were part of the closely knit team that created our holistic approach to medicine in our Mankato clinic. After she earned her Doctorate in Nursing at the University of Minnesota, she convinced Dr. Frank Cerra, then the Dean of the Medical School, of the importance of a center to expose medical students and doctors to integrative medical practices. Dr. Cerra was farsighted and he, too, could see the future of medicine. He agreed to take the necessary risks to fund the center at the university. He is another example of a man who was influenced by the women in his life. Not only did he have Dr. Mary Jo Kreitzer persuading him, he also had a wife and two daughters who said, "Get with it Dad, this is where medicine is going to go!"

The Center for Spirituality and Healing, started in 1995, now has several areas of focus: They are concerned with educating health care professionals on integrative health topics, empowering consumers, and impacting health care policy and reimbursement.

Currently, I do not have a clinic or center from which I operate. I consult with physicians who want to expand into a holistic practice. I also teach courses for physicians at Kripalu, a yoga center on the East Coast, and in various medical schools around the country.

Realizing the need for heart centered practitioners to support one another and to learn from one another, I have operated, for 23 years, a local Minnesota Holistic Medicine Group. Now that I have more time, our group has grown from about 20 or 30 members to 430 of us. There are 220 physicians and 210 other practitioners such as naturopaths, dentists, psychologists, chiropractors, and others. I organize a local conference every four months for this group; I have coordinated 58 of them over the 23 year period of our existence. We used to gather in living rooms, and now we meet in conference halls.

So, my commitment to integrative and holistic medicine continues to be a passion for me. I continue to believe the heart of medicine is in listening to patients and learning about their lifestyle and their habits. The heart of medicine is in helping patients understand what their wise bodies are trying to tell them about their lifestyle and the factors that are making them ill. The heart of medicine is to find ways to empower patients to address those factors so they can live healthy and happy lives, free of expensive and powerful medications.

How I stay True to Myself

For a physician, it takes courage to say, "Every new patient, I'm going to take an hour, and in a followup with that patient, I'm going to take 30 to 34 minutes, even if it's an OB visit, I'm going to take 15 minutes." Of course, the Mayo Clinic does this pretty routinely, and it is a major reason why I believe they do such good work. Many of the bigger clinics want doctors to take just 5 to 10 minutes for an OB visit because you see a woman every month and it's basically very routine. But I wanted a chance to sit and talk a little bit so I could know my patient. I earned less money because of that, because physicians are paid based on the number of patients seen. This was OK for me because both Diane and I made a decision that we didn't need a lavish lifestyle. From my perspective, doctors make a very nice income, and it is not necessary to set time guidelines so we make even more. It seems to me that doctors who rise to the top are highly competitive. We're used to winning. We win in sports, in grade competition, we get the positions we want in medical school and residency, and then we get out into practice, there's no contest any more. There's no way we can win, so then we start looking at salary: my salary is bigger than yours. From my perspective, how could it possibly matter if you're making a $100,000 or $120,000 or $300,000 or $330,000? It's like a baseball metaphor. "I don't care what I make, but I want to earn more than any other second baseman in major league baseball!" That somehow seems to prove that they're the best.

I suspect that it was easier for me to make some challenging decisions that I made because Diane had taught me to open my heart. My own life became more conducive to good physical and mental health when I was true to myself and when I nourished myself with healthy relationships. I believe that my work as an integrative physician and being a bit outside the box of being a "normal" physician was easier because I had prepared myself for this work and these decisions in different ways at different times in my life.

At times I've done meditation or yoga but my main practice has always been about my lifestyle and it is twofold: One is being in relationships that felt openhearted, honest and intimate, and two is trying to always be holistic which comes from the root word meaning healthy, holy, and whole.

In a healthy relationship, I get support from my friends. My life has gone through many changes and challenges and my friends sometimes make me uncomfortable and challenge me to grow, like my wife Diane did many years ago. With Diane, I became more than I was before. Sharing my life with friends whom I trust, who accept, understand and support me, reduces the anxieties that cause stress and, at the same time, my good relationships cultivate a sense of well-being and emotional security and I feel nurtured, loved and nourished.

Two, understanding my path in life, and having the good fortune to be able to follow that path prepares me for my work and life. I find that job stress can be a cause of chronic stress and chronic illness. Following my heart and my own professional and personal path has always helped me to manage the stressors that are natural for all people to experience on the job and off. Following my path leads me to greater wellness and happiness. When these two needs are met, good relationships and following my path, it's pretty easy for me to be open hearted in my practice.

I've always loved my work, I loved my patients, I loved the people I was working with and I didn't have to do much to feel open hearted. I'm not saying I didn't get rushed, or that time constraints didn't affect me. I had my finger in too many things. I would get time depleted, and when I got time depleted, I'd get irritable and not so open hearted. So I had to work on that.

Every day I walk outside; maybe four days a week in the winter, and not when it's too icy. About half the time, I walk with someone and have a heart to heart conversation. When I walk alone, that's my meditation time, it becomes a sort of a walking meditation, and it's my nature time. I make sure I get outside into nature because I've learned when I'm in nature, I am renewed, I relax, my mental clarity is revived, and I am more healthy, both physically and mentally. When I'm alone, I really exercise; I walk fast and I may alternate walking with running. I stretch every day, I eat in a way that's connected with the earth. I tend to eat a mostly plant based diet. I'm what Michael Pollan calls a "Flexitarian." I eat anything anyone wants to prepare for me. When I do my own food preparation, I tend to eat a mainly plant based diet. I'll eat fish or meat, though, I'll eat anything. I sing whenever I can, I dance, I avoid music or movies or books that feel toxic to me. These are all things I do to keep myself heart centered.

Every now and then, I get away for a week or so, and I learn new ways to renew myself. I just returned from a week retreat in Molokai. The topic was the Healer Within. Who are we inside. We did a lot of Shamanic Journeying that included lots of breathwork. There was music and drum playing that facilitated entering an altered state. We learned basically to bring the unconscious to the conscious. It's like dreaming, suddenly, your unconscious becomes conscious, but you are more awake than dreaming. I have trouble remembering my dreams, but I have no trouble remembering these journeys. You process your experience with a group and the whole week is totally heart centered.

I stay connected with quite a few good friends. I stay connected with my family, and my kids, and my grandkids. I stay connected to myself. I keep learning and growing. That is how I have stayed true to myself and I feel lucky and glad that I have at times had the courage to make the decisions I've made during my career in medicine. Although my decisions have kept me swimming up-stream, they have kept me true to my heart, and they have enabled me to bring my heart to medicine, to my patients and to my life.

Be True to Yourself

I would like to finish this essay by imploring people: If you are going to a doctor who parents you, doesn't listen, who doesn't help you look at your lifestyle issues, who puts a rope around you and says you are non-compliant, who treats everyone with certain symptoms the same, find a new doctor. You may have to pay for certain treatments that your insurance does not cover, but you will be a more healthy and happy person, and you will have a relationship with your physician that nourishes your heart as well as your body!

In addition, I would like to ask doctors to listen to your patients. Even if you do not feel you can make a whole hearted commitment to holistic medicine, I want to assure you that listening to patients can give you many new ideas and avenues for engaging patient participation in their own healing process.

Leading From Any Chair
by Cynthia Heelan PhD

Although many important lessons about leading with heart are already described in my chapter on *Finding Heart,* several leadership lessons of self mastery are significant for me as well. This chapter is titled, Leading From Any Chair because I have found that any individual, in any position, who lives from their heart can influence the environment where they work.

Focus on Strength and Appreciation

Early in my presidency, severe criticism arose about a very powerful leader who reported to me, we shall name him Dean. Many high level people reported to Dean, and several of those people came to me in confidence, one by one. They spoke in hushed, confidential whispers. They described their fear of retaliation for ever disagreeing with him. Retaliation came in the form of quiet decisions that squeezed them or others. Perhaps they would receive an impossible schedule. Perhaps a special fund for their campus would mysteriously disappear. With great confidence, staff arranged for me to meet with Dean and describe the criticism.

Over lunch, we sat down together. Confident in my ability to be kind and yet clear with him, I leapt right in to describe the concerns of others, without any words of support or respect for his competence and his many accomplishments. His face pinched, his hands disappeared under the table. We finished lunch without any small talk, yet he appeared agreeable to making some changes as we parted.

Before long, however, it became clear Dean was acting to protect himself. He garnered his power, frightened the people reporting to him, demanded to know who had told such lies, and turned staff against me. At meetings, an easy repartee with staff shifted to a frigid and hostile undercurrent. It took me some time to connect the dots and realize what was happening. At one meeting I asked openly, "What happened here? We were working so well together?" One courageous person said, "At this college, we have a tendency to put new people on a pedestal, then we throw rotten tomatoes at them." There seemed no direction to go with that comment, the meeting continued rimmed with frost.

Finally, Dean asked me to meet with him and his subordinates. I breathed into my hammering heart; held my trembling hands together, hiding my fear in my lap. At the meeting, all those who had spoken to me and asked for my help, were silent and sullen and impenetrable, afraid of retaliation. Dean reiterated the concerns I had shared with him, and he demanded to know who had told such lies to me. I managed to get out of the meeting without incriminating anyone by simply saying I could not do so.

Lurking in the back of my mind were the data that the average presidential duration for a woman was three years; for a man, seven years. It occurred to me, however, mine could be one of the shortest term presidencies of record, if I didn't do something fairly soon. I fretted about it, thought about it and, I'm sure acted pretty defensively. Some time passed, and I continued to worry and search for solutions. An interesting inkling appeared in a surprising place.

As a new Colorado resident and a person who loves jewelry, I was longing for turquoise, and on a business trip to Santa Fe, NM, I looked for a turquoise necklace. I walked into a shop and picked up the most beautiful piece. It was made with 20 small, turquoise, stylized bears strung together in a long necklace. The cost was exorbitant. I kept longing, "I want this necklace." Not affording it, however, I kept putting it on and taking it off and tried on other, less expensive necklaces. Finally, the manager, who had been observing this tableau, walked over to me and said kindly, "You really want this necklace, don't you!" I breathed "Oh Yes!" He ventured, "Well, I think you are supposed to have it. So I'm going to sell it to you for my cost." I gasped in surprise and delight, paid the price, hugged the manager, and left the shop before he could change his mind. I walked right over to Santa Fe's historic Plaza and the state's oldest art museum, built in 1917, and home to more than 20,000 works of art, including Native Art. Without consciously thinking about it, I was searching for meaning in this necklace.

I searched in the museum for the meaning of the bear in Native philosophy. I found it symbolized **unconditional love**. Dean came immediately to mind, "Oh, oh," I brooded, "What does this mean for me?:" It definitely felt like the gift was intended to be a message for me. Wearing the necklace fairly often, I continued to worry about what to do next for some time. I definitely did not know what to do. Someone reporting to me, had more power than I did with the staff reporting to him, and it was a ferocious, negative power.

One night, as sleep evaded me, I again acknowledged my lack of knowing what to do and implored the darkness for help. I awoke, startled, in the middle of the night. For some reason (I now believe my heart was guiding me in response to my openness, my "not knowing"). I stumbled out of bed, turned on the light, and, ever guided by books, walked over to my bookshelf. I simply reached up and pulled out a book by Sinetar. I opened it to this concept: When you are in conflict with another person, do not focus on the conflict or on their weaknesses. Focus on their strengths! Be positive! My breath caught, here it was, the message of the necklace, my key to unconditional love. To this day, I have not been able to re-find that quote in Sinetar's book! I only know that is what I read, that night.

The next day was the annual holiday party. Wearing my bear necklace, I walked into the warm lights and cheerful greens of holiday decor. People were ebullient, playing games and relaxing in holiday mode. Staff greeted me with jovial good humor, and holiday music softly framed the background. I looked for Dean and found him speaking with several of the people he supervised. I drew a deep breath into my throat and stomach, brushed my necklace while walking toward him, and gently touched his arm.

He looked down on me with alarm as though he feared a negative scene. I said, "Dean, I just want to thank you for the exciting curriculum developments and the new faculty discipline committees you recently created. I feel like we are truly on a roll now with innovation. Thank you so much for your quick action and your accomplishments." He, a foot taller than me, grasped my arm and deftly escorted me to a quiet corner. Out of ear-shot and in view of the entire room, he said, "You feel better about me, and I feel better about you too." Essentially, I gave Dean unconditional love and from that moment on, things got better and better between Dean and me, and meetings lost their icy glaze.

At his evaluation later in the spring, Dean observed, "I don't know what happened between us during the past year, but I really like working with you now." I asked, "May I share with you what happened from my perspective?" "Yes, PLEASE," he murmured. I divulged to him my journey around my relationship with him, my discovery of my bear necklace, and my middle of the night insight.

We began to use our experience together to illustrate how appreciating the value of others can create a community of trust; a milieu beyond just a place to work. Later we created a leadership award called the Bear Award. We gave it to those who worked to build community throughout the organization and demonstrated unconditional love toward their colleagues.

As I reflect on this life altering experience, I realize it contains aspects of self mastery necessary for leading from heart that both of us evidenced at that time, and that I wish I could always achieve.

Knowing my purpose in life gives order and meaning to it, Years ago, my stepdaughter asked me to describe my philosophy of life. I responded quickly that I saw myself making life as peaceful and happy and full as possible for those in my sphere of influence. She replied (having recently studied this concept in high school social studies), "How very 50's of you," I continue to be grateful for my upbringing in the 1950's and my persistent pursuit of doing my best for the world in my sphere of influence. This backdrop for my heart bolsters my ability to keep seeking for ways to resolve conflict in a loving manner.

Knowing my values helped me to make the difficult decisions both to confront the retaliation and to resolve the conflict. Being clear about my personal values helped me be open to creative ways of, for example, resolving conflict when it challenged me. Yes, I made many mistakes in my approach to leadership; I made decisions that had unintended consequences. My only basis for a clear conscience, was the knowledge I acted on my basic values,

Telling myself the truth about who I am, including overcoming my fear, helped me to manage my shadow anxiety and prevent it from casting its darkness on others, permanently. When I do not take the time to be conscious of my total self, (my light **and** my shadow), my actions and expressions tend to be from my ego and not from my heart. How many times as a college administrator and as a faculty member, I found myself defending some action for fear I would appear weak, indecisive or inadequate. My ego took over, and my sense of my inner self flew off to some place where I could not connect to it. I found myself de-valuing the thoughts and work of another, when all the while I was really questioning my own. I'm grateful, in the story above, I was able to reach out to the darkness, and into myself, for guidance.

100

Listening in a new way to others is part of my self mastery. Sometimes called **deep listening**, it requires truly SEEING another person, and then acknowledging my appreciation for what they do, who they are, and their impact on me. This kind of appreciative listening, both to myself and to others, creates an environment safe for dialogue and safe for an individuals to speak from her heart. This kind of listening honors the heart of the leader described above, and portrays a genuine desire to value her contributions to the organization.

Discipline is crucial to self mastery. Yoga, running and other daily exercise, reading poetry and reflecting on it, journaling, and meditating are a few examples of a daily kind of discipline. In maintaining a discipline on a regular basis, I have learned to support my growth in authenticity. Work to acknowledge my ego and affirm my physical body is an essential preparation for my leadership roles.

When I am able to live these lessons in self mastery, I am more able to be in touch with my heart, I gradually act from that place more and more. I can truly extend myself to others in a way that portrays my sense of service rather than control, and in a way that comes from my heart rather than from my ego. This has a powerful impact on others, and it is imperative, as both a model and in creating a safe space, to holding space, for others to speak from their hearts.

Holding a Safe Space For Ourselves and For Others

Parker Palmer: When we understand solitude and community, we also understand what it means to create a space between us that is hospitable to the soul, a community of solitudes, where we can be alone together.

Christine Schenk: It is important to stand, always, with both energy body and physical body feet firmly on the ground. When energy body "flies around" people often seem unfocused and jumpy. When both physical and energy bodies are unified in a loving partnership, things shift within an individual and within a group of people. New perceptions are possible, because information is energy.

Otto Scharmer: Presencing is retreating and reflecting, allowing the inner knowing to emerge. You access your own source. So you go from the chaos of observation to the still, inner place where knowing comes to the surface.

Peter Senge, Otto Scharmer, Joseph Jaworski, Betty Sue Flowers: Presence is being fully conscious and aware in the present moment. It is deep listening, being open beyond one's preconceptions to a larger field of awareness.

Learning to create a hospitable space for myself and for others, involves being completely grounded, listening carefully to myself and to others, loving myself and caring for others who share space with me. Learning to understand that this holding space allows the highest future possibility to emerge, has been the most important lesson of my professional life. These awarenesses occurred relatively late in my life, beginning at the age of 60. If you asked me now, what is the most important ability or characteristic for a leader, my answer is: The ability to hold a hospitable space for myself and for others.

This principle of holding a safe space seems to be emerging from many different fields and directions at the same time. Christine Schenk teaches energy workers and others who are interested in understanding and working with energetic issues to hold the space. Parker Palmer teaches those who would facilitate retreats for teachers and leaders and other professionals seeking their own inner wisdom to hold the space among them. Otto Scharmer and Joe Jaworski and Peter Senge and Betty Flowers support individuals in presencing, so they can be more present to the creativity that wants to emerge among individuals as they create organizations that make a difference to the future.

I learned from Christine Schenk, a teacher from Germany, that, like many people, I allowed myself to frequently be "out of my mind" to "fly around". That is, to be unfocused, to drift off into reverie, to lose my attention span, to not remember things that happened even though I was physically present. I could sit in a meeting and my thoughts were planning the next meeting. Meanwhile the current meeting could begin to veer off, people could begin to get irritated or angry, and chaos could emerge. It never occurred to me that my "flying around", my internal state, could have an influence on these external circumstances.

A powerful example of the power of being completely present with both energy and physical bodies came when I was working with a colleague, Jim, to organize a planning event for an entire college. We were using Appreciative Inquiry as a process, and my friend Jim was to be a co-facilitator who could help me observe and support positive group behavior in this large group planning session.

Jim and I were also friends, although I was fairly unhappy with his approach to friendship. He had flown to St. Paul from New York City, and we were having dinner in my home, after our planning session. We began to have a fairly intimate conversation about our lives and our work. He tended to act like he wanted to be my friend, intimate emotionally at times like this when we were together, but when we were apart, he never called or acted like there was any connection between us. If I was in New York and called him at the last minute, he was usually available, but if I tried to plan ahead, he would never commit. "That is not a good friend," I suggested at dinner that evening. "A friend reaches out, a friend returns calls, a friend makes time for friends."

"NO!" he shouted, and his hand slammed my dining room table so the dinner plates rattled. "That is not a friend, that is a lover. I am not your lover, your expectations are unrealistic for a friend," he bellowed.

I could feel myself begin to rattle like the plates, and shrivel and waffle toward my usual approach of going numb and escaping energetically or "flying" when confronted by this kind of behavior. Suddenly, I remembered to ground myself and hold the space for myself and for my colleague. I actually GRABBED space. I grabbed hold of myself and sat with both feet on the floor and felt for feeling in my feet. I put my hands on my thighs and felt for feeling in my hands and thighs, and sat solid so I could actually feel my bottom on my chair. I sat tall and relaxed, and I could feel my energy almost dive back into my physical body. I could feel both my ears and the top of my head as well as my feet, and, very important, I felt a loving feeling for myself and for my colleague.

The air around us transformed. I felt a richness in the air; I felt surrounded by a warm, golden light, and I felt gentle. Jim stopped in mid thought and stared straight ahead, silent for a second or two. He slowly pulled his slamming-hand off the table and dropped it into his lap. Finally, he looked over at me, his demeanor changed, and he changed the subject. I let the subject change, because I came to the realization that this was not a good relationship for me, neither friendship nor professional. There was no need to pursue this topic further.

We made it successfully through our consulting gig, with me working mightily to hold a loving connection within myself and for everyone else in the room, including my colleague.

As I reflect on that experience, I realize how different things might have been for me during my 33 years in meetings, that sometimes became especially negative and hostile. How calm things might have become when I had bosses who got lost in their power and role and dominated me or berated me in public. I learned I had within me the ability to generate a "field of energy" that calmed the space between myself and others. I began to realize that my relationship with the Vice President, Dean, years before, improved, because I was unknowingly appreciating Dean and understanding his needs as well as my own, or "holding the space between us."

More than once, when I was facilitating a planning process, again using Appreciative Inquiry, I found holding space to be a powerful and life giving influence for the planning work of an organization.

Sometimes it can be difficult for small groups to engage in the planning process. Usually groups of six are seated at round tables. The organization doing the planning has staff that arrange people in groups so there is a mixture of personnel: administrators, teachers from diverse departments, support staff, maintenance staff, etc. In one instance, a table of men from similar and same programs managed to gather at the same table. They clearly had not engaged in the question at hand, which was: Find, as a group of six, similar themes among the stories of success you just told one another. Their group of six had broken down into groups of two and three. They were not jotting down themes on large, colored hexagrams provided for this purpose. They seemed to be having separate, private conversations. I walked within 20 feet or so, of the group so I could unobtrusively observe the interaction. At first, I began to feel an irritation at their dismissal of the assigned task. Suddenly, I realized I was being negligent, and I needed to hold space for this group in a special way. I stood relaxed with my feet planted firmly on the floor so I could feel the bottom of my feet. I felt my hands and my ears and the top of my head. There is an experience while doing this, of feeling energy within my physical body; it is energy body moving within physical body. It is the process of becoming grounded. Then, I felt immersed in a great compassion and warmth toward that group of people not accustomed to this kind of dialogue. Within a few moments, they turned toward one another, and all six people began talking to one another and jotting down themes on their big, colored hexagrams.

I realized again, how important it is for a facilitator and for leaders and for all group members to stay grounded and feel present to themselves and to the members of their group. When many people hold this space, the impact is even more dramatic.

Other ways of describing the experience of holding space could be that of host. A host or hostess moves around an event seeking to make people feel welcome and comfortable. She radiates a sense of welcome and warmth. A classroom teacher transforms the energetic space in a classroom by how he loves the group of students. He speaks with compassion and empathy for different children and creates wide ranging learning modes for students with varied needs and abilities. In so doing, diverse learners feel safe and are able to work skillfully at their own pace and depth. A facilitator for a circle of trust encourages certain group norms, principles and practices (described fully in another chapter in this book). These norms honor the inner needs of group members, and help to engage every member of the circle in the deep listening that "listens" each person's inner teacher, into being present.

A leader can be such a host. It is important to note that the LEADER in this context can be someone sitting in ANY CHAIR. Anyone and everyone possible in meeting spaces can engage in hosting, caring, safe and warm behavior. While greeting people into meeting space, a sense of welcome and warmth can prevail among those who understand, not just the person with the leadership ROLE. Individuals who are not the designated leader, can make it safe for different viewpoints by modeling that behavior themselves. Individuals can encourage everyone to listen carefully to one another so that the best ideas and wisdom of a group can be harvested.

This caring behavior, of any group members, can be done verbally. It can also be done by individuals who sit quietly, grounded and caring for the entire group, speaking their truth when it is desirable, and accepting the truth of others in the true sense of dialogue—That is, holding the space, for self and for all.

In their book, *Presence*, the authors describe their interview experiences with organizations. When individuals entered a state of deep listening, of being open beyond normal preconceptions, the field shifted, and the forces shaping a situation were able to shift from doing the same old behaviors to realizing something new.

More Tools for Creating Space for Others

Appreciative Leadership

The personal preparation for leadership that comes from self mastery, self growth, from speaking from the heart, and holding space, opens the way for others to speak from the heart in our organizations. Most of us hope, when we join a community, we will engage with our colleagues around issues of substance. We all aspire to the profound aspects of our fields and to the mission of the organization, and we expect to talk with others about them. We hope to build on our own knowledge and to create something wonderful together. Too often, we become caught in the mundane—the tangled web of funding, profitability, accountability, and the vagaries of rapid change. A leader is tempted to become directive, to function from her mind instead of her heart and to neglect the hearts of her colleagues. On the other hand, the hearts of colleagues can appear to be rigid and unwilling to change and innovation appears to be stunted. While it is real that mundane issues are important, and while it is true that some hearts can be unwilling to change, there is also another reality.

The other reality is, many employees would welcome the opportunity to engage in a dialogue where they could bring their hearts and their energies and their contributions to increase institutional vitality. In workshops I have conducted in many parts of this country, administrators and staff have expressed this desire. If they believed they could actually make a contribution to a more authentic life within the institution, and if they felt they would be appreciated for their effort, staff would participate in conversations of substance and consequence. When we, as leaders, genuinely appreciate the contributions of others it is evident, and colleagues feel safe to speak from their hearts. It is the leader's role to create the environment and to organize the space so that dialogue around both the meaningful and the mundane can occur.

Creating an Appreciative Community

In an appreciative community, people appreciate one another! Creating an appreciative community involves bringing together a group of diverse individuals who are free, in a safe environment, to speak from their hearts about the things that matter most to them. The phrase appreciative inquiry, developed by David Cooperrider, connotes a strength-based approach to leading an organization. When I appreciate my colleagues, I identify what they are doing right and then build on those positive resources to create meaningful and enhanced results. An appreciative approach increases organizational abilities to improve, strengthen and foster collaboration.

Providing information is one way to appreciate people. People change when they feel a need; when they are so moved by new information they give up current beliefs and are willing to create new meanings. In addition, every living system chooses whether or not it wants to change. If people do not believe what is being said is important, they ignore the desired change or they may even undermine it. These tendencies could be called benevolent neglect or malicious compliance. Sometimes good people in an organization are ready and willing to do good work, contribute their ideas and take responsibility and leaders hold them back.

An example of good people being ready and willing to contribute and take responsibility, occurred for me during my presidency. As a college, we implemented a key strategic initiative around helping students succeed at social interaction and personal growth, as well as retention, graduation and transfer to four year schools. We hired consultants to help identify our service gaps; everyone in the college worked to develop campus-based plans to bridge those gaps and we set quantitative goals for increasing student completion, graduation and transfer. After several months, I was surprised and delighted to discover a group of dedicated individuals had self-organized around enrollment management. The team traveled to all seven campuses on a regular basis to initiate dialogue, identify areas where they might support and assist and to bring a college-wide focus to each individual campus's student success initiative. In fact, freshman retention increased from 45% in 1996 to 58% in 2001. I felt proud and so excited at this creative activity.

To my embarrassment, I have also been part of that other kind of leadership. In the late 1990's when on-line courses began to burgeon, we administrators told our faculty to refrain from offering any courses over the internet until the college determined it's "particular niche". In truth, faculty members quietly added on-line components to their courses and surreptitiously prepared for full on-line courses long before administrators were ready to support the concept. This could not exactly be called malicious compliance. Perhaps it is devious or creative compliance! Looking back, an appreciative dialogue with faculty and valuing everyone's expertise and contribution, could have moved the college very easily toward cutting edge use of technology.

Sometimes when resistance to change occurs there is a feeling among staff that if there is a need for change, then they must be doing something wrong, There is consequently a common defense used by people—all people are the same—they resort to face-saving tactics in the threat of embarrassment. The behaviors may differ with varied cultures, but the "theory in use" is the same—save face! "That study was flawed," or "Those data are not accurate because the study did not include (you fill in the blank!)." One solution is to bring people together around information and assist them to understand the need for action, and the need for acting together. The message is: Create communities of shared interest and common concerns. At the same time, an appreciative approach to sharing data can also be vital.

I have discovered it is also possible to **use data in an appreciative manner by** gathering data illustrating how well an organization is doing in some areas. Appreciative information can truly create a community of support and a community of trust. An organization is energized by building on a successful past, for an even **more** successful future.

Creating a Community of Trust

As mentioned above, communities can organize around shared meanings, values, goals, desires and plans. Discovering shared interests changes relationships and people; old grudges can get left behind, and people can seek out one another to get help for their interest. Meaning motivates people, and leaders are in a position to create situations where people can create their own meaning, when they have an opportunity to organize around their shared interests. Leaders create opportunity and time for people to talk together about why we do this work. People need opportunities to engage with one another and share their information with one another—across groups rather than only in their own departments. When those opportunities abound, different people see different aspects of an issue, and new ways of approaching any issue can arise. Information belongs to everyone, and purpose belongs to everyone, and choices made are those which many can support.

There are many techniques for organizing communities of meaningful dialogue, or communities of trust. A few large group approaches to dialogue include: Appreciative Inquiry, Future Search, Open Space Technology, Strategic Conversations, World Café, and Real Time Strategic Change. All approaches that assist colleges to create safe communities of trust, like mindedness, and shared meaning. Each approach allows for individual and community inclusion, greater innovation, resolving long-term issues, and generating institutional vitality.

Another opportunity for creating a community of trust is shaped by Parker Palmer. In this kind of Circle Of Trust, all staff come together to support one another in their efforts to listen to, and to hear their own hearts or their inner teachers speak. Faculty and staff at many colleges, and doctors and their staffs are coming together to read poems and chapters and to dialogue about the feelings and meanings they evoked and consequently, the things that are most meaningful in life. They tell their stories and ask one another honest and open questions. All these activities assist the shy heart, to make itself known and to speak. Another chapter in this book describes more completely, Circle Of Trust.

Organizations engaging in this kind of Circle Of Trust are experiencing a burst of vitality, productivity and excellence. Again, Richland College, a member of the Dallas County Community College District, is an example par excellence of a community of trust. Staff members participate in Circle Of Trust retreats, form many different kinds of dialogue communities and in general have an appreciative environment for all constituents of the college. In 2006, Richland College won the prestigious national Baldridge Award for excellence in education.

Richland College exemplifies leadership that opens space for conversations that need to happen, creates a climate of possibility and innovation, even in the midst of change and anxiety and brings the right people and the right conditions together to engage around complex problems.

Conclusion

If we are to truly create and maintain institutions of vitality and creativity, there are required elements. First, a leader needs to understand the source of her strength and vitality, her heart, and then she needs to be brutal about mastering her shadow. The source of our shadow is our ego. The source of our vitality and creativity is our heart. Once the leader has begun the journey to experience and act from heart, for it is a journey not a destination, he can begin to create an appreciative environment where **others** can be safe to explore and express their hearts.

Since the journey is arduous and difficult it is tempting to say, "Oh really, this can't be done."

However, what it takes is commitment—commitment to self-mastery, to living from our hearts and to engaging others. Once a leader is committed to the journey, a flow develops. People begin to "get it," and a community of dialogue forms. When leaders surrender to their own hearts, they exert an enormous attraction—not because they are special, but because constituents are attracted to authentic presence and to a future that is full of possibilities. Once we are committed, events flow from the commitment. All kinds of things occur in our favor; unforeseen incidents, meetings and material assistance, of which no leader could have dreamed, come our way. Goethe has said, "We are attracted to what is already ours in secret. Thus passionate anticipation transforms what is indeed possible, into reality."

Whole People Create a Whole Organization and Whole Communities for a Whole, Healthy Planet: Richland College

by Steve Mittelstet PhD

The bees pillage the flowers here and there but they make

honey of them which is all their own Montaigne My life is my

message.

—Gandhi

Now—as President Emeritus of Richland College—I have the luxury of reflecting on the rewards and challenges provided me through the nearly one-third century I served as Richland's President and the nearly four decades I enjoyed as teacher-learner there from when it opened in 1972.

I began to see the connection between Montaigne's bees and my own learning-doing when I first read his 16th-Century Chapters in one of my undergraduate French literature classes. The connection stayed with me throughout my leadership career and remains with me today as I watch bees cross-pollinating Calendula with Basil flower and lacy Chervil blossom from the rocker on my kitchen deck in rural wooded East Texas and from the fifth-story communal patio garden of our downtown Dallas efficiency high-rise, the two very diverse communities in which our lives—mine and my partner Guy's—now cross-pollinate in "retirement."

I also learned early in my Richland career that Gandhi's inspiration, true for the individual, is just as true for institutions. I saw it was especially true for Richland College. There, we collectively over time set our institutional vision for the college to be the best place we could be to "learn, teach, and build sustainable local and world community", characterized by "social equity and justice, economic viability, and environmental vitality." In short, if how we educators were conducting our own lives and the teaching-learning processes of our institution was at odds with what we were professing, our observant students would intuitively feel and cognitively observe the hypocrisy. They would see the irrelevancy of our vision to their world and quite likely apply whatever they learned there more or less randomly throughout their lives rather than with sharp focus on building sustainable local and world community. Educators, especially, must do our best to model the change we want our students to make in the world. We need not only to speak authentically from our hearts and minds but we need also to walk the talk from our hearts and minds.

To what extent were we—students, faculty, professional support staff, administrative leaders—successful in creating a culture at Richland College that offered the appropriate balance of support and challenge to help one another lead authentic lives consistent with and appropriate for achieving our institutional vision?

"Imagine a school that has a soul" opens the video narrative shot in 2005 on Richland's campus by an energetic team sent to "capture on film the heart of Richland College" shortly after the White House and the Department of Commerce named Richland the first community college recipient of the Malcolm Baldrige National Quality Award. This was only the third time our nation's highest award for organizational performance excellence across all sectors of business, manufacturing, and service organizations had been presented to an institution of higher learning. In one short day of videotaping on our campus, our insightful visitors had captured themes of mind-body-spirit connection; vibrant, honored spirit of place enhanced by current "inhabitants" of the campus; engaged learning; a strong sense of purpose; thoughtful conversation; responsible risk-taking. They saw it as all wrapped up in something often summed up by students and employees as the "Thunderduck Spirit." R. Mobius Thunderduck (aka "Moby Duck") is the name of Richland's mascot. More than a mascot, it long ago became synonymous with the importance of nurturing the inner-self, as students and employees learned to experience the Mobius-like connection of our inner lives in activating our outer lives of service to other individuals in supportive community with one another, our planet, indeed the universe.

What caught the critical eye of Baldrige examiners with regard to Richland's performance excellence—as measured and sustained over time with increasingly impressive data-supported student-learning outcomes connected to Richland's vision—was Richland's insight that it takes whole people to create a whole organization. We knew that Richland had to be safe for people to bring their whole selves to learn, teach, and work every day. We needed to ensure that processes and systems would not break down and cause our inspired bees to fail to perform their roles well and, worse, even to be punished for what very well might have been an institutional failure, not their own. In organizations where people do not feel safe to take responsible risks to innovate, try something new, ask what otherwise might be judged as "stupid, irrelevant" questions, people will not expose their souls to painful judgment. They will, instead, learn to disengage, become isolated, and depend on their rational selves to determine how to "play it safe." They will learn to "go through the motions," "get the paycheck," "get the grade," while leaving their souls at home. Moving on as soon as they can, looking for a place where they can more authentically "connect soul-to-role," they leave behind soul-less organizations.

Like diligent Thunderbees stealing from this flower and that, however, Richlanders discovered through inspired professional development how to engage in meaningful, thoughtful, non-hierarchical conversation and dialogue with self and others (in contrast to the too-often bellicose debate-to-win-the-argument communication approach so prominent in academia). In those conversations, they discerned that not only minds but souls can and must be nurtured in our educational institutions, in concert with healthy bodies, if we are to be our best as learners, teachers, and active community builders. In other words, we learned that an academic institution can help whole people develop—especially our wildly and richly diverse, often extremely needy, community of learners. And without whole people at Richland, we determined we could not create and maintain exceptional core systems and processes to provide maximum desired student learning success results for all our hard work, even sometimes exceeding our wildest expectations. We began to observe the interdependent, integral Mobius phenomenon at play once again, this time with whole people, whole organization, whole community, whole healthy planet.

Learning to Speak and Act from Our Hearts

Whole-Person Circles of Trust.

Richland invites its employees to participate in a variety of "Whole-Person 'retreat' series" throughout their Richland careers. These series of varying lengths and formats are conducted by Richlanders who have learned to facilitate such series through the Center for Renewal and Wholeness in Higher Education (CRWHE), which is also headquartered at Richland College. Facilitators use "third things", such as poetry, art, and physical activity, to help each participant engage her/himself in the safety of a supportive, trusting community that holds a place for participants individually to delve more deeply into their inner selves; to ask non-leading questions to help a focus person find his/her own answers; and to interact without attempting to fix or advise. Individuals learn to confront and gain deeper understanding of both the shadow and light within themselves. They get deeper insight into the impact the necessary interaction between the two Mobius-like characteristics, light and shadow, have in their authentic lives and, in turn, the impact the interaction has on others, especially our students and their learning. We learn that once we are more comfortable with our own authentic behavior, we can better help our students become more authentic in their learning—through our curriculum, our "classroom" student-learning behavior (whether on-campus or via "e-learning"), our student development programs, and our other student programs, services and campus operations.

Important outcomes of these inner reflection series include going about our days more reflective about what occurs around us and our own reactions thereto, "turning more often to wonder prior to judging" what occurs in our environment. In difficult leadership situations at the college, I frequently marveled at the interplay between my own physiological and emotional behaviors as I would "turn to wonder" at myself and then at the "other/s" when my blood pressure would rise and my adrenaline would begin to pump. When I would take a few nano-seconds to deep breathe while reflecting on why my physiological state was losing balance, I was better able to let my rational self help me play an adult role in approaching the situation. Sometimes seeing myself in previous similar, emotionally-charged situations during one of these brief breathing-reflecting episodes, I could consider whether my own issues were filtering my hearing. I could then frame a much calmer non-leading, non-judgmental question for clarity to bring myself and the other party/-ies into meaningful, caring conversation rather than lashing out emotionally or doing a poor job of attempting to be rational by pretending to ask a non-judgmental question that might trigger similarly volatile response/s from the other party(ies).

Throughout more than a decade engaging more than 250 Richlanders in these wholeness and renewal series, the culture of Richland College for our students and our work colleagues (a sizable critical mass in an employee base of some 1500 full—and part-time employees). In my role as College President, I also conducted quarterly orientation sessions for all new employees where we reflected on how their "fresh eyes" could help them and other Richlanders live out our organizational "ThunderValues," which include most of the CRWHE-inspired attributes described above.

Richland's Thundervalues and the Touchstones of the whole-person development series have become more and more intertwined over the years. Touchstones are a set of behavioral norms that guide conversational behavior during the wholeness series. They include behaviors like deep listening, being completely present, identifying assumptions, speaking our truth in a way that does not judge others, and turning to wonder prior to judgment. Even as we review college data related to our monthly performance excellence targets, we turn to wonder prior to judgment when the data are not what we expected, asking good questions that can keep our organization data-informed, without being data-driven. Outside of wholeness series sessions Touchstones continue informally to influence more civil, mindful conduct of many of our faculty and other staff meetings in which much of the college business is accomplished.

Richland's Thundervalues for student and organizational behavior were forged more than two decades ago through dialogue among students, faculty, staff, and community advisors representing business and industrial workplace interpersonal skill needs. The values follow in summary form: "Because we believe it is the whole person who best teaches, learns, and builds sustainable local and world community, we affirm these organizational values in our interactions with one another: Integrity; Mutual Trust; Wholeness; Fairness; Considerate, Meaningful Communications;

Mindfulness; Cooperation; Diversity; Responsible Risk Taking; and Joy." Reminders of these values (Thundervalues in Action) greet employees daily as they turn on their computers at work. A "pop-up" screen features one of the ten values and remains the greeting all week long. A photo example of the value in action at Richland illustrates the greeting, inviting everyone to incorporate that value in that day's activities and to report exemplary instances of the value at play to the editors of the Thunderbridge Employee Newsletter in the "Thanks, Thunderducks!" column for everyone to enjoy. Once the day is underway, various council and staff meetings precede their agendas with brief recent illustrations of the featured value in action on campus. Opening "business" meetings with such moments of college-related appreciative inquiry help participants focus positively on the agenda at hand and on one another as whole persons, especially in dealing with potentially divisive issues. A fundamentally different and more genuinely productive meeting ensues from this approach than from the many other, frequently dysfunctional meetings that occur in many organizations.

Intercultural Competence

More than 60% of Richland's diverse student body of ethnic groups are historically under-represented in U.S. institutions of higher learning; the employee ethnic "mix" is similar. Such diversity provides rich potential for creating a curriculum and an organizational culture for learning how to lead productive, rewarding personal lives while simultaneously helping build sustainable local and world community. However, since most individuals do not usually acquire intercultural competence through the normal course of growing up or in their formal education, Richland has developed an on-going professional development curriculum that helps employees assist one another and their students improve their own individual and collective intercultural competence as an important lifelong skill. All Richland new employees participate in a basic six-part series during their first three years of employment. The series is designed to help participants continue to improve their levels of intercultural competence and communication skills. Following completion of the basic series, all employees continue their intercultural competence learning throughout their Richland careers by participating in a minimum of three hours of annually changed, theme-based professional development selected and offered by Richland professionals.

Cooperative Learning as a teaching-learning "classroom" approach is a methodology taught to all Richland full-time faculty throughout their first three years at the college. They, in turn, teach the methodology to Richland's part-time, adjunct faculty (80% of whom at any time have participated in the sessions). Cooperative learning approaches minimize the use of lectures, emphasizing instead student engagement in their own learning and with their classmates—lifelong learning skills that are more commonly needed in places of work and other "real-life" situations. Imbedded in this learning methodology are critical-thinking and active-listening skills, collaborative problem-identification/solving abilities, and, critical to Richland's mission and vision, community-building skills.

Clearing minds and emotions for learning

In our employee wholeness series, we frequently ring a chime at the beginning of each session, followed by an extended period of silence, to bring participants into the present after a break or following other activities of the day. A number of faculty participants—finding such an approach helpful in focusing attention in the series sessions—have devised their own ways to begin classes in a manner that helps students clear their minds and hearts from the realities of their busy (and often extremely challenging) lives, thus helping the entire class to be more fully present for their learning with one another and their professor in the upcoming class. Some professors actually use a chime in a manner similar to the manner it is used in the professional development series. Others sometimes use a 3-5 minute focused writing designed to help clear away everything that has preoccupied students prior to arriving in class to be more fully present by focusing on the learning topics at hand. Student end-of-class evaluations make it clear that this manner of starting class is well-received.

In addition to these methods to help students and employees learn to speak and listen from their hearts, as well as from their minds, other activities help Richlanders live out their ten Thundervalues. A number of these include the many planned and spontaneous rituals that foster joy, trust, and community—in and out of the classroom—such as periodic college-wide "13-minute laugh breaks," parades to honor outstanding employees, college-wide student and alumni recognition celebrations, and other rituals to encourage spontaneous "fooling around" to maintain a spirit of joy in the midst of Richland's hard work at teaching, learning, and serving.

Physical Spaces for Speaking and Acting from Our Hearts

Throughout my leadership tenure at Richland, I felt it important that we all, students and employees, learn about, honor, and contribute positively toward the "spirit of place" that historically emanates from the physical campus that now houses Richland College. This history (including prehistoric activity there) is part of the orientation that both students and employees receive at Richland College. As part of honoring the campus that we all inherited, everyone is invited to consider the impact their presence on that site will have for those who follow. To what extent will what I do here enhance the heritage? To what extent will it diminish this rich heritage for those who follow? A variety of college-wide rituals help remind us all of how our presence adds to the campus's spirit of place. More important, Richlanders teach one another a vital life lesson about life on this planet. Will how we live our lives enhance the spirit of place we inherited during our stay on this Earth or will it diminish it?

The immediate previous existence of what was to become the Richland College campus was a many-generation farm situated on nearly 400 acres. To honor that history, as part of our second-decade celebration, we created a Founders Arbor at the site of the most recent farmhouse, the debris from which had been removed when original college facilities were built in 1972. The only remnant of the farmhouse was a concrete slab covering the water well where the hand-pump had been located—a rather shabby reminder of what had been. So, we also re-established the well with a functioning hand pump—a remarkable likeness to the one we saw in a family photograph we received from the most recent farmers. The well, which originally pumped water from the historical McKamy Springs via Ferris Creek, long ago provided water for local Indigenous tribes and their horses before the farm was built. Still today the springs and its creek, as it did before human life appeared in the region, provides water for plant and animal wildlife as it works its way to White Rock Lake and onto the Trinity River that runs through the City of Dallas and several of its suburbs.

Richland feels a sense of custodianship for McKamy Springs, which becomes Ferris Creek, which now travels in underground culverts far beneath the City of Richardson, which long ago buried it and built neighborhoods and businesses on top of it. The creek re-appears above ground on Richland's campus, just inside the northern border of Dallas, and is transformed into what are now known as Upper Lake Thunderduck and Lower Lake Thunderduck. These two "lakes" run through the center of the campus, the east and west sides of which are connected by three pedestrian bridges, including a two-story one, which also serves as the main student interior passageway across the lake to each side of the campus. This central glass-walled bridge passageway and central student lounge, which is connected to the Student Center Dining Room, provides full view of both levels of the lake, as the Upper Lake cascades over a major dam waterfall, which flows under the passageway bridge to create the Lower Lake. Hence, numerous Richland metaphoric references linked to our life-enhancing mission draw on the life-forces of water, such as the Thunderwater Organizational Learning Institute (the name of which stems from the powerful roar of the falls throughout the campus during and following rainstorms) and on bridges, linkages, and connections, such as our Thunderbridge Newsletter. In addition, all Richland buildings are named for historical Texas bodies of water—names fairly equally divided among Indigenous tribal languages, Spanish/ Mexican-named sources, and English, for those European immigrants who died in the Texas' Revolution with Mexico prior to the land being formed politically into its own Republic and then becoming the Lone Star State whether in the Confederacy or the United States. Each building name also has a mnemonic connection to the primary purpose of the facility. For example Spanish-named Guadalupe Hall—referencing a major Texas river—houses the Gym. Wichita Hall—named after a prominent Texas tribe and Wichita Falls—is the primary generic classroom building on the West side of the campus. Bonham Hall—named after a prominent Alamo soldier and his namesake Lake Bonham—houses the School of Business.

Founders Arbor still includes the pomegranate shrubs and the ornamental arborvitae cedar-cypress conifers that once flanked the farmhouse porch. Horticulture students built a split-rail fence to shelter gardens they designed and planted with Texas native flowers. Richland Facilities Services employees installed a brick-paver floor under the Arbor and a brick walkway for honoring employees who would complete 30, 35, and now 40 years or more of their careers at Richland College or in combination with other colleges within the Dallas County Community College District (DCCCD).

Adjacent to the Arbor is the TLC Labyrinth (TLC, for Teaching, Learning, Community Building). Participants in our many wholeness and renewal series before long determined that as Richland's pastoral campus enrolled more and more students and was becoming more bustling, the campus could benefit from more places for students and employees to step away from all of Richland's busy-ness for a few minutes for quiet reflection and rejuvenation. And so Richland employees and students raised funds to install a sixty-foot diameter outdoor walking labyrinth, using tall wavy native grasses and native limestone as the pathway dividers. Adjunct faculty, realizing mobility and sight-challenged individuals would not be able to navigate the physical labyrinth, purchased a beautiful all-weather finger labyrinth so that these individuals, too, could experience the reflective serenity of this historic space. This quiet get-away on the banks of Upper Lake Thunderduck beneath the shade of a grand native pecan and lake cypress canopy has now provided thousands of students, employees, and community members from early morning into late in the evening a place to tap into and contribute to Richland's spirit of place as they re-charge their own souls, so that they might speak and act more authentically from the heart of a whole person.

Richland's Carillon resounds throughout the campus and adjoining neighborhoods quarter-hourly. Its origin, which followed that of the labyrinth by a few years, emanated from the same source: wholeness series participants who felt a quarter-hourly simple bass-resonant chime would provide yet another reminder for us to connect our souls to our campus roles, taking brief time-outs throughout the day, wherever we might be on campus, to reflect in silent gratitude for the opportunity to fulfill our teaching, learning, sustainable community-building calling on Richland's beautiful campus. Every time I heard the chime, I personally delighted in the lovely paradox that the quarter-hour gong simultaneously caused people to fret about lost time and the need to hurry up while, for others, it was a reminder to be in the moment, savor it, and give thanks for our personal and institutional missions on this campus with one another and our students in a community of mutual support, which we hoped would serve as a model for a life well-lived long after each of us had left the campus.

These are but a few illustrations of the many other spaces that provide Thunderducks an opportunity to renew souls and build on Richland's spirit of place, enabling those who participate to speak and act more authentically from the heart as well as the mind. Such spaces include reflection gardens, meditation rooms, outdoor classrooms, picnic tables, park benches, wildlife/nature habitats, interior art galleries and outdoor sculpture, combinations of xeriscaped and more formal gardens, fountains, bridge overlook seating areas, cantilevered lakefront decking, and trees, walls, and walks with plaques honoring longevous service and memorializing lost loved ones—and, more recently, the new LEED-Platinum and LEED-gold designated Sabine Hall science building and nearby Garland Campus.

Processes to Ensure Performance Excellence

Although I believe everything described so far in this chapter is essential to Richland's performance excellence, most of what I've described has probably never entered the minds of most of the taxpayers who expect Richland to give them a good return on their public investment: educating students in a productive amount of time to ensure that they complete sound educational goals, whether through transferring to a university to further their education, completing a job-ready certificate, or gaining new workforce skills in an ever-changing economic job market—and being successful in whatever that next phase might be. In short, they expect performance excellence and may well have never considered the role that whole people might play in that accomplishment, even though Richlanders see it as a too-often overlooked key to the smooth, productive running of any organization.

Some two decades ago—serious about our "organizational business"—Richland College embarked on a "continuous quality journey" by, among other things, forming (in conjunction with the DCCCD) a nation-wide consortium primarily of community colleges, now known as the Continuous Quality Improvement Network to which it still belongs. Actively participating in this consortium throughout the years led Richland to begin adopting elements of what would later evolve into a comprehensive "performance excellence" discipline related to the Malcolm Baldrige National Quality Award (MBNQA), which was created by the United States Congress in 1987 and continues to be overseen by the U. S. Department of Commerce, which in tandem with the White House, presents the annual award/s (there is no set number per year; however, 2-7 awards have been presented annually since the MBNQA was first conferred in 1988). Designed initially to inspire the improvement of U. S. global productivity, primarily in large and small businesses and manufacturing, it later expanded to encompass service organizations, most notably health services, followed by education, and most recently non-profit organizations. Most of the fifty States have their own state awards and related training and oversight based on the seven criteria provided by the MBNQA. During Governor

Ann Richards' tenure what is now known as the Texas Award for Performance Excellence (TAPE) was established. I and several of Richland's executive leadership team (ThunderTeam) received training as TAPE examiners to help us determine whether this might be a comprehensive discipline to engage our entire operation in the achievement of our mission and vision. Hesitant at first—especially since neither MBNQA nor TAPE had criteria specifically designed for educational institutions—we nevertheless knew of no other state/ nationally supported comprehensive approach to increasing our performance excellence, so we launched on a nearly two-decade long "journey" by taking what has arguably proved to have been a "responsible risk."

In a nutshell, the seven criteria of the MBNQA help guide an institution to direct ALL its resources to its primary mission (ours remains "teaching, learning, community building," which eventually has come to emphasize sustainable local and world community as we have grown more proficient at understanding the interconnectedness of all that comprises our planet and universe and our role in helping our students learn to live responsible, productive lives in community with others. That means that all Richland's processes, systems, programs, services (and the people who "operate" them) must be unwaveringly aligned to enact our mission and realize our vision through ever-improving four-part ADLI cycles of improving strategic and operational Approaches, Deployment, Learning (measurement), and Integration (integrating the learning into the next improvement to increase results). Although Richland was honored in 2005 by both the Governor's Office (TAPE) and the White House (MBNQA) with our state's and nation's highest awards for performance excellence, that was never an ultimate goal. In many ways, however, the awards may have provided a reassuring boost to launch a more robust spiral in our ongoing quality journey. As a result, Richland College is a much higher performing institution by virtually every measure today than it was in 2005—even in this current challenging post-recession socio-political-economic world attempting some semblance of recovery. The MBNQA discipline is about continuous and breakthrough mission-related organizational success in an on-going, sustainable fashion. It serves as a guide in our own journey, not as a destination to an award.

It is gratifying, in my still-new Emeritus status, to see that the leader-full Richland organization continues with remarkable performance excellence now that my three decades of leadership have concluded. Still confronted with the frequently asked question, "What's the key to Richland's success?" (Someone's always on the lookout for the one quick "silver-bullet" to success, a phenomenon perhaps endemic in at least American society), I respond with something like, "The key seems to be Richland's long-term, on-going actionable belief in and commitment to nurturing whole people as lifelong teacher-learner-community builders to help our students learn to be even better at it than their educators, who are willing and eager to follow a performance excellence discipline throughout their Richland career to help Richland achieve its lofty mission and vision." It's a mouthful and frequently a conversation-stopper, as it sinks in with people I have not provided the silver bullet they might have been seeking. And then, I quickly add to the remaining few in the conversation or audience: "But the good news is there are many more performance excellence journeyers with us now and we're all eager to share benchmark information with other eager co-learners on this journey. We're not out there on our own like we were in the beginning."

Leading Richland College from the Heart

When I accepted the invitation to write this chapter, part of the invitation included responding to the "who" questions inherent in Richland's wholeness development work: "Who was the person who served as Richland's President for so many years and who is he now post-presidency, as an emeritus?"

I was an engaged student-learner from the beginning and probably always will be. As Richland's President, I wanted to continue my learning, my personal and professional growth with my colleagues both at Richland and throughout an ever-growing network of professional colleagues and extended family. What better type of organization to lead than one full of master teachers? Most organizations have to pay big bucks to bring expert teachers to train their employees. In our organization, teaching-learning was our business. I was surrounded by master teachers who not only did the work but taught others to do it as well. I determined early on that if I could be as successful leading our college in its mission as our master faculty led their diverse community of learners each semester with just the right balance of challenge and support, making "just-in-time" adjustments in their approach for individual learners who needed something more, something different—and to do it with such joy—I, too, might have a shot at success as their Chief Thunderduck. And, thus, I set out on a path that included "hanging out" with Richland's master teachers, sometimes team-teaching with them, soaking up all I could that would both address my ever-present student-learner needs and my needs to learn to be the most responsible servant-leader I could be to help them continue to grow in their own work. And the joy of it all!

I think, as relative youngsters in the '70's and '80's, together we Thunderducks had a reasonable modicum of success under this simple-minded leadership approach. We certainly had a lot of fun!! And I think our largely college-ready, largely ethnically homogeneous student body of about 3,000 students in the early years were reasonably successful. Without any data to back it up, we had lots of anecdotal accolades that fed our egos and early on built a surprisingly strong academic reputation for this new community college surrounded by public and private colleges and universities in North Texas.

I had always been a highly successful student, in terms of GPA at least, and was successful in any job or assignment I had attempted. Perhaps self-driven to success in the face of a challenging father-son upbringing, I was perhaps too much a believer in the pull-yourself-up-by-your-own-bootstraps school of my first-generation immigrant family father. Since I had not personally experienced anything that looked like failure to me well into my young adulthood, I was not terribly patient with, nor nurturing of, those I considered whiners or long-sufferers in Richland's employ. Unless they were under my direct supervision (and I frankly didn't think we had all that many), I just let their supervisors deal with them and, again, "hung out" and got inspiration from the high achievers at the college. Although not a recommended leadership strategy, I think I lucked out with this strategy, as some of the wiser and more experienced master faculty for some reason took me under their wings and quietly led me to learning experiences that benefitted my leadership and, therefore, the college in aligning with its mission to achieve its vision.

The turning point for me personally was that it was a group of these same faculty who convinced me (it didn't take all that much for these folks at that time to convince me of most of what they suggested, such was my trust in them) that Richland needed to embark on a journey which would nurture the development of whole people (authentic people deeply in touch with their integrated mind-spirit-body—but using very different language at that time). As with so many Richland innovations and creative initiatives, I wanted to be among the first to participate, both for selfish gratification and because I wanted to witness first-hand what might warrant longer-term investment. My participation in the whole-person programs at the heart of this chapter—to the point of becoming a CRWHE facilitator years back and now remain a National Distinguished Advocate thereof—helped me in all the ways it has helped so many others at Richland and in the 40-50 other institutions of higher learning where CRWHE has nurtured facilitators.

First, the reflective series helped me discover that I, too, have a shadow side and that in my role as College President, that shadow could have disproportionate impact on the college, its students, its employees, and the communities it served.

I've encountered my shadow over the years as well, and I know how that shadow casts itself over the college and causes dissension and concern. I once had a very good idea with a good rationale. The idea was about a need for more people at our college to work year round, including faculty. Since we are open year round, the nine month agrarian model doesn't always work for us. My idea was to have teaching/administrators. Teachers would be hired to teach half-time and then they'd administer some area connected to their area of teaching expertise half time. I thought we'd have a fair number of these across the college especially in areas like coaches, music directors, and program developers, and recruiters. Often the people who were hired to do these things as faculty members got tired of doing them and focused solely on teaching, and the other aspects of their responsibilities dwindled. Our system was such that a faculty member could make that change, and then we'd hire part-time people to do the programmatic things.

My change idea had so much good about it, I didn't build ownership around the concept or use the idea as a sounding board. So then it was a defiant act, particularly to the faculty on our other campuses who feared it could destroy the whole faculty history and culture. It was not honoring them and they would not be included in the faculty meetings. My thinking was 'only if they chose to exclude themselves'.

After a time, I decided I would do this in spite of the sit-ins I had in my office and so-on, and we did. We hired very good people. The irony is, because they were good people, and because our faculty members are responsible and open, people helped them to be successful. They were also very angry. They lost trust in me and feared maybe I wanted to do away with faculty all together—all those dark kinds of thoughts people have when they don't understand what's going on and you seem to be behaving in a way that's not consistent with what they know. I said, "You know this is a pilot" and was defiant, and it went on for several years.

We hired maybe 20 individuals to do the administrative work half time and to teach half time, and finally it came to a head with faculty leaders from around the district saying, "You know you're putting these people in an awkward position. We don't really understand it, we don't see that it's causing a lot of harm and yet it's not good.

You know we don't want to do those things in the summer, we're glad to have somebody here doing it, and we don't have to rotate through it." That was exactly what I was after because things got kind of rugged in the summer and we lost productivity, service, and secretaries were advising students.

So someone I respect from another campus and several of my faculty leaders sat down with me, and we worked out a way to get out of the impasse by re-labeling these people and I promised to never again use the words 'teaching administrator'. We now call them coaches and program directors and associate and assistant deans and they continue to teach part time.

If I had handled things differently, we could have accomplished the same thing without the defiance and conflict. I realized in doing our retreat work, there is a part of me that gets into a competitive mode or "I will show them; I'll do what's right whether or not they know it" . . . all that dark, shadow sort of stuff. My ego became a part of that and caused it not to be as successful as it could have been. It was a heart-breaker for me, and it broke the heart of some of my closest faculty colleagues who came to me and said, we need to move on from this and put ourselves back together. It was a very emotional and mutually supportive kind of time. I was fortunate there were faculty who wanted to help me because that could very well have been the end of my tenure at Richland. I was heartened that a culture we had built over time helped us through that period. I was reminded of my own humanity and that I need always to be vigilant about doing what I'm doing and to sooner than later own up to that as opposed to denying it.

Paradoxically, if I let my personal light shine so brightly that it cast a shadow over other high performers responsible for our collective successes, that also was problematic. It was in these retreats that I personally learned the art of not fixing, of asking non-leading questions (first, of myself, and then of others), of turning to wonder prior to judgment, and so many of the other elements earlier described in this chapter. These experiences helped me be more understanding of the challenging lives all people lead, including myself, and helped me be more open personally to receiving the support I often needed from the trusting, largely self-leading college community which was beginning to emerge. I think it was not an accident that as I became more nurturing of my own whole person, I was better able to help the college do the same for its employees and students, for if those working with our students are broken, it is less likely they can help our students with their brokenness.

My personal mind-spirit-body nurturing daily ritual usually began in some sort of quiet outdoor space that involved walking, breathing, stretching, and being with myself and my surroundings, reflecting, observing, especially inside myself—whether in the woods down by the creek by my home, five houses off the campus, on the campus well before classes would start, or later on city streets well before early morning traffic started when we moved to a high-rise condo in the heart of the Dallas business district, where I discovered numerous quiet parks with beautiful water features and art throughout. By then, I had learned how to tap into the spirit of place in about any situation in any location, taking energy from it, and attempting to enhance the spirit through my brief presence for the benefit of others who would be there after me. My native American flute frequently accompanied and soothed me on these meditation walks. I continue this type of ritual as part of my early morning re-charging routine, as well as throughout the day, as I did when I was at the college. But now I and my partner diversify our living-learning experiences in post-DCCCD life spending about half our time in residence in downtown Dallas and the other half in the rural East Texas woods, in both of which homes we continue to devote our lives to building sustainable community in both our sharply contrasting local communities and globally through the little Fair Trade enterprise we have begun with a collective of Guatemalan women whose business started with micro-loans, as well as with an international Board of Trustees on which I serve for the Institute for American Universities in southern France. In each of these endeavors, which also include two non-profit organizations, we see analog opportunities to nurture whole people in developing whole organizations in these very diverse communities that can nurture one another in numerous ways. Who knows, these two non-profits might soon launch a whole-person Baldrige performance excellence journey before long!

In the meantime, we are delighted to find that Gramps and Pops have important, rewarding roles to play as nurturer-learners with our two pre-school grandsons and infant granddaughter and our adult children who parent them so well.

Conclusion

Obviously, many factors and experiences have converged to help Richland College develop as an organization with soul and spirit actively engaged and aligned in on-going performance excellence in achieving its student-learning mission and vision to be the best place it can be to learn, teach, and build sustainable local and world community. It remains a co-creation of Richland faculty, staff, leaders, students, and the communities served by the college and which created and continue to support the college. I firmly believe that Richland will long be a joyous hive of Montaigne's bees continuing to make a honey all their own in whatever local and world context it finds itself and it helps to shape. I also believe Richland's life, like Gandhi's, will be its authentic message, the message it purports to be. I personally continue to strive in my post-Richland life on an unpredictable, fascinating, sometimes waddling, bumbling journey that was immeasurably enriched during my career at Richland College. May my life be that of a superb honey-making Thunderbee that continues to learn how best to conduct an authentic, meaningful Moby-life, the message of which is as harmonic with the universe as a bee-life can be.

Authenticity and Leadership Integrating our Inner Lives with our Work

by Paul A. Elsner PhD

Now I become myself. It's taken time, many years and places.

I have been dissolved and shaken, worn other people's

faces.N.B.—May Sarton

What is Authenticity

Authenticity may be one of the more elusive issues I've been thinking about for some time. For several months, I attempted to work and rework an appropriate language for explaining what I meant by "authentic leadership." One mantra that sticks with me is one I inadvertently coined in working up a chapter for one of Terry

O'Banion's books about learning colleges. The mantra is "Leaders learn; learners lead." To be a learner first, and a leader when called for, places you in a better mode for authentic behavior.

One could argue that much of administrative leadership is perfecting a dance, perhaps many disguises, or worse, adopting a persona for each occasion or interest group. Let's offer that as the opposite pole of authentic leadership, but what is the other pole? Paraphrasing Parker Palmer, *it is, perhaps, an exploration of the self, the self filled with both light and shadow and the willingness to explore both, and the courage to keep one's heart open when it is most difficult that is the mark of an authentic person.*

Current Authenticity in Higher Education

In the academic community, we strain under the conventionally accepted coda of objectivity, empiricism and the scientific method. Such important foundations of the academy, as they are, do not let in the emotional, the subjective, and the intuitive processes that often really guide us through life. It is as though our emotional points of view, and our passions contaminate the objective, detached approach of the empirical method.

An outline of the conditions higher education faces at present could be helpful as a stage for understanding what is needed. The scenario could go something like this: American Higher Education seems to foster and sustain a serious disconnect between its substantial momentums and its enviable place in the world with the very students it purports to serve. Many of us think that higher education has an obedient, even obsessed, student clientele that has little passionate attachment to its tasks. For the graduate student in a competitive research-I university, it might mean:

> I don't wholly believe in all of this, and I don't even question the integrity of what I am required to do, but I will stick it out, because that is the game they play here, and the stakes are too high for me to stand out by questioning too much. I just hope I get out of here intact personally—whatever that means—because I sure

as hell am all but ruined financially and my self-concept isn't very high either! Why my misery? Why my pain? Could there be something else?

A community college student holding two jobs, attending school at night, piecing together a quality moment with a spouse and children, doesn't know how to find an inner balance, much less a spiritual, kindred outlet. Stress, financial breakdowns, family disconnect all scream at her; he is the Edvard Munch character ready to break on the bridge.

What do we do to students' love for learning when we ask

them to remove personal experience from their work?

We have seen our students love their learning, find their passion in literature, in the arts, and in other studies. But the questions for me are: Who is reflecting on what our students are coming to know when they must deconstruct, jargonize, and analyze their subjects to the point of lifelessness? What are we doing to that love and passion when we ask students to remove all personal experience from their work?

A while back at Wellesley College, Parker Palmer addressed a national gathering of over eight hundred people who had come to participate in a conference billed as "Education as Transformation: Religious Pluralism, Spirituality of Higher Education." Parker's words seem appropriate here:

The dominant pedagogy in higher education today is objectivity and analysis. The problem with this pedagogy is that it is untruthful to the way that we come to learn. We have come to know this through our personal association with the subject. Unfortunately, we are guided away from the intuitive, subjective ways of knowing because such behavior may spill over on the subject to be learned, thus, fouling or contaminating it.

While our tenured administrators and faculty are impressive in the scale of their enterprises and commerce, our students feel less and less connected to us.

Turning the market forces in our favor is more dazzling. Higher education seeks to transform itself to these new market forces, but with each ratchet-up of this transformation, more student anomie or obedient inertia builds to massive disconnect. The energy may be impressive, but there is no moral compass present, and many fewer value checks about what this being market-oriented is all for.

This may sound pretty melodramatic, but when Robert Bellah wrote *Habits of the Heart,* he gave us a portrayal of a core study of adults who could not find their galvanizing purpose in life, even after successful professional careers! Our students would look like Ballah's core student case studies in extremis, if we were to revisit them in twenty years. This does not have to be so.

The Inner Journey

It does not have to be so if we can look within at our "inner landscape" as Parker Palmer calls it, and begin to lead and to teach and to be students in a different, more heartfelt way. This search this can lead to challenges in language as well as in deed.

In working with Monica Manning of the Nova Group, the larger struggle with language became apparent—sort of like hitting the wall. Manning's work with me found her offering a careful paper that she called "The Language that Invites Inquiry." Manning offered that our language should be inviting, evocative, exploratory, respectful, and concretizing. It should be inclusive without being insipid. It should help us hold ourselves accountable. It should be appropriate to our purposes and to the academic work place. Monica emphasizes the importance of language on individuals as well on the institution as a whole.

> When we focus on individuals, then our language should encourage people to explore how they create more integrated, holistic lives in their work places. When we focus on institutions, our language should foster work places that support faculty and staff using their talents in ways that provide for productive and rewarding professional and personal lives.

At Maricopa when we explored authenticity, the "s" word [spirituality] gave us no small trouble, for understanding self does suggest a life of the spirit. We reasoned that the language of spirituality would be "off-putting" to many and inviting to some. Our secular society builds walls to keep out such language that suggests spirituality's role, especially at our workplaces. Yet it is the absence of our own awareness about our "inner-landscape" that prohibits true connections with each other. We may agree that it is the spiritual life that we mean when we refer to "the inner life." We may acknowledge that a diverse set of spiritual traditions can enrich our understanding of this inner life and the ways to connect it with our "outer lives." We may even find ourselves growing in comfort with words that have traditional religious connotations. Still, we run the risk of using language with which we, as a core group have become comfortable because we have struggled with it, while the larger group that we want to invite into dialogue is put off by the same terms. Concern for language is real and it is important to be as inclusive as possible in talking about the inner life.

Inner Journey in Higher Education

This inner life can be applied to teaching as well as to leading and to teachers and to students as well as to leaders. Sandy Desjardins, an English instructor at Scottsdale Community College, has made a powerful point about teaching writing. She maintains that students write with more power and expansiveness if they allow emotions in. Good writing can materialize from exercises that focus on writing perfect topic sentences, but when students are engaged, even passionate about their subject, writing comes more naturally, is likely to be more expansive, and carries a deeper message to the reader.

In team-teaching with a colleague in China, I found that Chinese students, usually terribly reticent about branching off too much with English, became more expansive and adept writers when they could tell about the defining moments of their lives. It was being granted permission to "tell their stories" that brought them to more confident writing and expression. This experience has led us to conclude that one cannot effectively teach English to the Chinese with an approach that is limited to language mechanics, structure, and grammar. One must live the language. Language must be taught and learned by culturally contexting it, by personally contexting it, and probably, by spiritually contexting it.

For the Chinese with their guarded nature, such tapping of their inner spirit, their personal stories, is much harder for them than it is for us. But, we are convinced that such efforts of expression can uncover the authentic self for students faculty and leaders.

At the 2000 International Chair Academy, Sandy Shugart, a community college president, opened his keynote remarks by stating that leadership is often incorrectly seen as a perfected method or technique. Like Parker Palmer maintains, it is not technique alone that draws your students or your followers to commit to you in a teaching or leadership role. The students, like our co-workers, want to see you, to know who you really are—not to know every personal detail of your life, for this would be unbearable, but to see and know you as a person.

I have sought refuge in the writings of Margaret Wheatley for the forging of an "authentic rationale." If I sometimes can't get to authenticity by direct paths to the leader, I can envision an organization where the leadership and its members do not cancel each other out. Rather, some organizations create a chemistry, a dynamic, and an energizing spirit that seems to invite participation, creative risk-taking, a sense of personal wholeness for itself as an organization and all of its participants. Its leader may not be greater or lesser than its members in displaying such a healthful dynamic, but the leader is seen to be contributing and participating as much as leading. Wheatley may have captured such an organizational ethos and essence in the following description.

> Each of us embodies energies of life. We are creating, systems-seeking, self-organizing, meaning-seeking beings. We are identities in motion, searching for relationships that will invoke more from us. We bring these desires to our organizations, seeking from them places where we can explore possibilities. Our energy courses through our organization. This energy is the best hope we have for creating organizations that feel alive.

I credit Monica Manning, whom I cited earlier, for helping me create many signposts that could pop up like spring-loaded Peter Max cardboard cutouts to quell my fear and bolster my courage to walk an unfamiliar path in a very dark and unexplored woods. When I ask myself why we are in these darkest of woods, a Thomas Merton signpost warns:

> He, who attempts to act and do things for others or for the world without love, will not have anything to give others. He

will communicate to them nothing but the contagion of his own obsessions, his aggressiveness, his ego-centered ambitions, his delusions about ends and means and his doctrinaire prejudices and ideas. There is nothing more tragic in the modern world than the misuse of power and action to which men are driven by their own Faustian misunderstandings and misapprehensions.

Or, Margaret Wheatley advises—just in time at the most difficult turn:

> We encourage you to question yourself at the level of your beliefs. Such personal questioning requires us to go very deeply into our ideas about the world. It often causes us to challenge more than we want to have challenged.

Like Joseph Conrad's, Heart of Darkness, we journey where the most telling truths do not evade us, but stand out. Our pride, our egos, our self-esteem, our deceits are not hidden. And Parker Palmer puts his signpost in full view:

> True action, effective action, action that is full of grace, beauty, and results is action based on discernment of and respect for the nature of the other. The reason is simple: Only through such a relationship to the rest of reality can our action flow with the action of the Tao. Only so can we be channels for real power . . . [much] social action [is] action which does not respect the nature of the other, action which depends on human power and is perverted by human pride.

As a leader I find solace and support on this inner journey in the writings and signposts of others and in the knowledge that I either face my own ego and my shadows or cast that shadow on others as I function in my leadership role.

Application of Inner Journey

At the Fetzer Institute, several higher education committee members asked, "For all of higher education's outward, dazzling acceptance and apparent success, what is wrong in the kingdom?" Some of us were willing to say "A LOT!" But are there remedies at hand? It may get down to things as basic as training our colleges' colleagues. After all, we are dealing with the health of our organizations here.

At Maricopa Community College I helped form a group, broadly named the "Authenticity Group," probably for lack of any better candidate term. Since the group was multi-represented by several special interest, subject area, and employee groups, the assembly of the several persons provided a window on the Maricopa organization that I had not seen. I was surprised to hear that there was almost a longing hunger for employees to find greater meaning in their lives, some compass to greater life and career fulfillment. Group members spoke of longing for mutual connection. Some expressed that the pay was good, the jobs challenging enough, but something not so easily definable was missing in both their work and in their lives.

One of the central tenets of this group that was drawn from my suggestion came out as: If Maricopa could create an organization where all of its members would seek and find integration between their inner life and the work that they do they create an ever more dynamic, and ever more creative, and an ever more safe organization.

I have gone further to suggest a universal thesis; if we set upon putting together the right kinds of teachings, we could create a less woeful life for ourselves, but if we allow ourselves to play out ideal scenarios, we could avoid a woeful world and achieve a happy, more satisfying life.

Before you conclude that I have turned into a delusional mystic, let me tell you about some of the workshops we designed for our employees and faculty. With the assistance of many from the

Authenticity Group, we sought ways to bring these values to the college as a whole. Several workshops were created and were widely attended and they all presuppose the trainability of certain life skills. Here are the titles of some of these workshops:

- Divided No More—Bringing Your Whole Self to Work: Discover the importance of alignment between individual and organizational values.
- Personal Journaling—Learn how to use journaling to get in touch with yourself.
- Simplify Your Life—Discover and affirm your reasons for desiring a simpler lifestyle and clarify how you can move toward it.
- Natural Life Centering—Spend the afternoon learning and experiencingTai Chi.
- Brain Gym: Connecting with your Inner Technology—Explore "Brain Gym" to achieve goals quickly and efficiently.

Most of these workshops have required tight instructional design and solid facilitation. Again, I mention the struggle with language that occurred in the Authenticity Group. This search for an operational language seems to fall into place at times and to elude us at other times.

In our Authenticity Group, a problem we faced grew out of our insecurities about where the project might take us. I also had apprehension about issuing a wide call for participants in this discussion. The Authenticity Group became more open about fears of who comes into the tent. They feared that persons with their own religious agendas would slip in, and perhaps, be overly doctrinaire and inflexible. Once they reasoned that this was classically inauthentic behavior growing out of their own insecurities, they confronted their own shortcomings and did not seem to have a problem—such as they imagined it.

Finally, we struggled with the question of how much would be lost if this initiative became chiefly an organizational development project.

Would we lose our bona fide self-examination, our institutional soul or center or would we come to discover it?

Workshops on personal journaling, life simplification, life formation and centering, employee assistance, spiritual exploration and values' formation seemed to be the answer, and it seemed important to allow them to occur over a period of time.

Our Authenticity Group, such as I described, would work with faculty and staff development professionals to design and orchestrate a system of experiences, forums, workshops, and dialogues about the importance of nourishing our inner life.

Assessing Success of Authenticity Work

How do we know if these interventions change organizational climate and general health and well-being? Evaluators could search for instruments that might use the Likert scale and could be administered each year for two to five years. Hopefully, we could find movements on these scales of positive measures of well-being. We would define these movements in terms of our desired outcomes. The criteria could have the following residual effects.

* openness and safety;
* the ability to offer and consider uncommon solutions to common problems;
* the propensity to award interesting failures and bold experiments;
* a significant diminishing of stress syndrome:
* decline of cardio vascular disease,
* decline in grievances and conflict,
* decline in substance abuse
* the measures of life satisfaction,
* the incidence of creative innovation and personal needs and work satisfaction:
* job sharing,
* telecommuting,

- consultative leadership vs. role leadership (redesigning and renegotiating more satisfying work roles);
- central motivations derived from passion and caring for others;
- suppression of ego-needs,
- more collaboration; less competition, bonafide consultation;
- redefinition of power: power to interpret; listening power; the power of grace; the power of synergy; the power of fully developed human potential; the power of peak experiences at high creativity;
- the power of selflessness and projecting to other's needs.;
- a less divided self.

I have not ruled out an institute to train a national cadre of community college leaders, such as has been done with the National Institute for Leadership Development, the Chair Academy, and the Campus Compact Training Center.

Conclusion

In conclusion, I hope that authentic leadership, authentic climates and cultures can bring about the feeling and exhilaration of our work. Such peak experiences and exhilaration will occur only if we explore our inner life and connect it to the work we have chosen to do. This connection brings us to the authenticity we seek in ourselves and in others who lead.

Co-Creating Space for Heart at Work Using Appreciative Inquiry

by Cynthia Heelan PhD

Sometimes, we don't create opportunities for colleagues to gather together and co-create because we don't know how to make it happen. We are afraid of potential conflict, or confrontation, or we are afraid new ideas might arise we cannot handle or integrate into the real lives of our organizations. Conversations of substance are a process, and we don't know how to make a process work for ourselves. That is why a process like Appreciative Inquiry can be such a support to an organization.

Every individual in an organization has a story! We don't often know this story, because we don't make time to listen. At the same time, individuals don't see how their story has any connection to the stories of others in the organization. Appreciative Inquiry, as a process, encourages individuals to share their story and then to see how it fits with the stories of others to create a mosaic of successful actions in an organization.

Appreciative Inquiry is an approach inviting each member of an organization to share an important story of personal success within the agency, with colleagues. The story is one that comes from the inner heart of each individual's work, and as the process evolves, the entire organization is able to see how individual stories contribute to the entire organization's success story. Personal stories become the basis for creating a plan that builds on the success of individuals; they create an opportunity for every person to contribute to and co-create the future of their organization. In addition, the opportunity to share, to contribute and to co-create establishes the format and the momentum for continued trust, creativity and commitment. Specific examples from organizations using this process illustrate what happens in an organization when individuals are encouraged to speak from their heart.

A frequent and primary focus in organizations, is often that of problems. Organizations have communication problems, morale problems, customer service problems, financial problems, marketing problems and endless performance problems. We almost always focus on these problems, and they tend to be a weight on us and to worry us. The truth is, that for every problem we have in any group, there is someone, in some corner of the institution who is doing it right. There is someone who works with customers in a helpful and extraordinary manner. There is someone who communicates with clarity and transparency. There is someone who is a top performer. Not only are there single individuals doing things right most of the time, almost everyone in the organization does some aspect of all these problem areas well at some time in their career or at some time of the day. These are the places we need to place our focus. Instead of asking the question, "What is wrong with our organization?" We need to ask the question, "What is right with our organization?"

DeWitt Jones in his film, Celebrate What's Right With the World, describes his work as a photographer for National Geographic.

National Geographic, according to Mr. Jones, has as it's mission to send photographers to some of the most forsaken parts of the world and then directs them to find what is beautiful and worth celebrating in that part of the world. The National Geographic magazine speaks for itself in that regard. It is so beautiful, as Mr. Jones says, we can never bring ourselves to throw it away. In a similar way, we can ask our employees to tell us something they did right, something beautiful, something worth celebrating. Asking questions like this can encourage people to speak from their hearts at work. We can invite staff members to tell a story about what they did well in the organization. We can celebrate what is being done well, what is going well, what is right in our world in several steps.

So the first step is to pick a problem, any problem. Let's say our organization's most pressing problem is inter-departmental communication. As an Appreciative Inquiry devotee' my preferred approach is to gather ALL of an organization's employees into one room. Some have many employees in different places and so we have gone to several towns and worked with each employee group separately. Then we put the data from each site together.

However you choose to do so, once your employees are all in the same room, encourage them to sit at round tables of mixed employee groups. Individuals can be given a color or a number or some other code that marks their table site, and then they find themselves in a group with maintenance people, support staff, professional staff and others. This diverse mixture allows each person, when they tell one another their stories, to see evidence that everyone makes a significant contribution to the success of your organization.

Step two is to ask your question about what is being done right in the organization regarding inter-departmental communication. The question might be: "Think of a time when you were a part of or observed excellent inter-departmental communication. Perhaps you were part of a team that communicated an important action all across your organization, and people were thrilled and excited about the news. Or perhaps you simply were the recipient of information that made you feel good about other departments because of the information you received and the way you received it. Make this an exciting time; make it an experience that really made you say, "Wow. This is going to work. This is something to really celebrate!" "Think, too, about the circumstances that made the inter-departmental communication successful. Who were the people involved; what resources were made available?" Invite everyone to jot down a few notes about their experience; then invite each person to share their story with **one** other person.

A buzz goes up in the room with half the room speaking out loud. People become animated, their hands start telling their story, their partners start to smile, the story teller starts to smile. There is a positive energy that prevails, as 250 or 400 or 75 or however many people are in the room, share a story that deserves a celebration. Some story tellers feel heard for the first time ever in their organization. I have seen people tear up because it felt so good to have someone understand their work and get a sense of their accomplishment.

By the time every story is heard by a table of eight people, each individual feels they contribute something significant to inter-departmental communication, and the mixed group at each table sees how each person, no matter in which department they work, contributes to inter-departmental communication in your organization. They also see there are common themes among their stories. Energy continues to go UP in the room as each person feels heard and honored for their work, and the day is off to an exciting start.

The participants at each table of eight, work together to identify common themes in their stories. Each theme is written on separate large pieces of paper, then posted on a wall where everyone in the room can see them. The room starts to move as people from each table walk up to a wall to post their themes. As they post on the wall, staff begin to notice they are not the only table with most themes. Other tables have similar or the same theme. Everyone in the entire organization sees the importance of similar activities leading to interdepartmental communication! Consensus begins to form, organization wide, without having a loud or contentious discussion.

Everyone is invited to help organize the individual themes from tables into organization-wide themes. People over by the wall, point to themes while others actually move themes around to find the right "family" of themes. Everyone in the room either is actively engaged or stands back to see where "their" success eventually falls in the organizational scheme. Imagine 500 people (or 30 people depending on the group size) standing with their coffee cup and a pastry or apple, waiting to see THEIR story on an agency-wide wall.

The large group then is able to see that organization-wide, there are common elements present when people are at their best and communicating well across departments. These themes are highlighted. It is as though the employees have taken a microscope and zeroed in on all the right things going on regarding communication. The microscopic slide is then enlarged and overlaid on everyone else's slide, and all the pieces fall into a beautiful mosaic of successful behaviors, circumstances, and resources. The organization can now replicate, enhance, and build on these themes to become ever more successful at inter-departmental communication.

This is a good time to **have a genuine celebration.** Different organizations celebrate in different ways, but my favorite experience was the organization with 800 people in the room. First music resounded over the intercom, and people began to move their feet, some actually danced around the tables. Balloons were tied to chairs all around the room, Fresh coffee was served, and then a few staff wheeled in an enormous cake ablaze with candles. Everyone got a piece of cake, and then a video show began that highlighted some of the most exciting moments of the organization during the past few years. People stood entranced, waiting to see themselves on the big screen. Many, many people were filmed for this video. Then the CEO took the microphone and spoke to everyone about their good work and the great results they had all worked together to achieve.

She then announced the T-Shirt commemorating the occasion. After 30 minutes or so, the music dimmed, the leftover cake was wheeled out, and the next step in the process of Appreciative Inquiry began to unfold.

Step three involves table groups finding common ground and coming to consensus about their most valued success themes and any wishes or new ideas they may have. You might ask the question, "Come to consensus as a table of eight on which three to five themes, if you really placed an emphasis on them, could take us fast and far to being an organization with outstanding interdepartmental communication. Each table of eight identifies their top themes and posts them. Those themes are structured into organization-wide themes again.

Each table then selects the ONE theme they believe could take them really far and fast toward outstanding interdepartmental communication, and they draft a vision statement about it, building on what they have already accomplished.

A steering group of mixed employees later takes all the information, and they identify the top proposals, select the three to five they can address over the next bit of time (a year, five years, etc.), and they send their selections out to the entire group to approve. The most responsive organizations again use the Appreciative Inquiry process to further engage interested employees in building implementation plans for each initiative chosen.

One organization addressed the question: "What was a really positive teamwork experience you had or observed during the past year? Who was involved in the team? What were the circumstances surrounding the team that supported the results? All college staff (at five different campuses) told a story about a time when they felt particularly included and appreciated? How did the story happen? Who was involved? What circumstances helped to encourage inclusion?" After telling their stories, finding themes and deciding which themes were the most important to replicate and enhance, the steering committee culled seven major initiatives, and they stated them as a vision; as if the vision had already been accomplished:

The agency works together to organize organization-wide social events.

The agency implements awards in a way that inspires out-of-the-box creativity and appreciates unique talents as well as team efforts.

Recognition exists for valiant efforts that fail in order to cultivate risk-taking.

Staff work together to ensure success stories are shared weekly and divisions and programs are showcased.

We work to implement Appreciative Inquiry across the agency. This will help to ensure open dialogue, collegiality, and collaborative efforts.

The organization implements leadership development for all interested individuals so that strong leadership can emerge 'from any chair'. This will include facilitator training in Appreciative Inquiry and the work of Parker Palmer.

The college creates a DVD, celebrating the rich history and vital future, including the contribution of individuals.

When these themes were announced to the college, all those who participated in the event could see evidence of their input. They saw EVIDENCE that they had spoken with creativity and with passion, and TOP LEVEL LEADERS HEARD THEM; their recommendations were being accepted and implemented! The response was so enthusiastic, that over 300 people volunteered to help implement the seven new initiatives for inclusion, involvement and communication.

Volunteering staff were trained as facilitators, and they, with coaching, led the seven groups of people in creating detailed implementation plans using Appreciative Inquiry. The college continues to implement, assess and update their seven initiatives using the Appreciative Inquiry process.

Staff were amazed at the results. One astute leader jumped out of his chair in a meeting, "These are the seven major gripes we have in our organization, and no one ever complained!" This is one of the most exciting results of a process like Appreciative Inquiry. There is no need to find problems and assess blame for those problems. It is possible to focus on what is being done right, then discover ways to do more of it, and in the end, problems are actually addressed—without pain.

This wonderful example is replicated in organization after organization that uses the process called Appreciative Inquiry. People are engaged, people speak from their hearts, and instead of a brouhaha of anger and volatility, there is joy and communication, high morale and productivity. People see how their individual work fits into the organization as a whole, employees learn how consensus works and repeatedly use this tool, people see how they function when they are at their best, and they are able to see how they can get better and better at what they do. Appreciative Inquiry makes it possible for all employees to come together without complaint and to co-create their future.

One besieged organization leader called me after the first organization-wide event and cried into the phone, "You helped me change the morale in my organization in one day!"

**Touchstones support inner work
help keep participants safe**

Co-Creating Space for Heart at Work Renewal and Wholeness Circles

by Cynthia Heelan PhD

A Renewal and Wholeness Circle puts into practice the work of Parker Palmer, and enables a unique and empowering experience for an organization. Harvard authors Lee Bolman and Terrence Deal write: "Perhaps we lost our way when we forgot that the heart of leadership lies in the hearts of leaders. We fooled ourselves, thinking that sheer bravado or sophisticated analytic techniques could respond to our deepest concerns. We lost touch with a most precious gift—our spirit." Renewal and Wholeness circles incorporate reflective dialogue and conversation to regain a sense of spirit, of heart, and authentic voice, so that people feel able to bring their hearts to work in a new way.

Too often, mission-driven institutions treat their employees as instruments to manipulate customers or to achieve productivity goals, staff development events have that kind of manipulation as a hidden or overt agenda, and the workplace can become a disheartening place. Employees begin to hate staff development activities, conferences and retreats because they dread the latest new buzz being laid on them as an important new technique to improve productivity. Based on a decade of experience in organizations around the country, employees in a **completely voluntary** program of retreats for self-reflection and exploration, indeed can and do make a difference in their own lives, and in the life of their organization. However, the intention is the opportunity to engage in the kind of self reflection—in community—that allows a person's own inner wisdom to "show up".

This radically different form of promoting employee success offers a chance to spend time in retreat away from work with an agenda that is challenging, but not focused on methods or techniques, and there is considerable surprise, enthusiasm, and gratitude among participants. One participant from a business office expressed his surprise, "Retreats gave me a sense of my own creativity. I drew things, I wrote poems and I had no idea I could do that; I'd never done a poem in my life. I gained depth of knowledge about myself. I've become more alive." Comments like his are abundant among retreat participants.

Parker Palmer, in working with teachers in K-12 schools and with faculty members in community colleges, with doctors and other groups, created the concept Circle of Trust®. A circle of trust is a community of like-minded persons who use dialogue to prompt the ability to listen to one's own inner teacher (think heart). There is no fixing, no advice, no direct guidance, only the opportunity to explore one's personal truth as inspired by a poem or a story or a song. As we listen to the metaphor in a poem, for example, then listen to the truths of others, often our own heart opens and new insights occur to us and we are able to speak them to ourselves and to the circle. In this way our heart has been retrieved, we listen to it and we can be guided by it.

One important way in which a circle of trust invites a heart to appear is story-telling. Remember, our authentic self, our heart, came to us when we were born, so stories about childhood can be an assist in retrieving the guidance still available to us there. I will always remember the retreat, years ago, when we read the summer poem, Camas Lilies by Lynn Ungar.

> And you-what of your rushed and
> useful life? Imagine setting it all down—
> papers, plans, appointments, everything—
> leaving only a note: "Gone
> to the fields to be lovely. Be back
> when through with blooming."

As I heard the poem read aloud twice and then had an opportunity to reflect on it, I was suddenly overwhelmed by a childhood memory of my mother's peony bushes surrounding our sprawling back yard in Madelia, Minnesota.

Perhaps as many as fifteen peony bushes of pristine white and blushing pink, silky clouds of sweet fragrance, bordered our backyard. Mother had transplanted them from her mother's garden, from the family farm, and her mother had transplanted them from her mother's garden. Every spring, those peonies, with their irresistible scent filled our yard and then our home. Mother would produce her favorite glass vase. white glazed pottery shaped like a long, slender and elegant leaf, from its hiding place where curious children couldn't find it, and fill it with her beautiful, sweet smelling blossoms. The fragrance softened me; it drifted over my closed eyes while I drank it in. My sister and I would salvage a few of the puffy blooms and sit in the back yard and play with them, sensuous little girls, often using them to fill out our blouses, (in the years before we filled our blouses with our own budding flesh!).

In the circle at the retreat, the Camas Lilies became peonies, and they flooded me with loving and tender memories of the gifts of my childhood, my sister and my deceased, Irish Catholic mother, whom I didn't always remember as a giver of gifts. I instantaneously knew why I always had fresh flowers in my home, and why, when the season for peonies came around, I felt so loving and peaceful and robust, and went in search of peonies. This childhood memory opened my heart wide to the gifts of summer and my mother, and I was ready for my inner teacher my heart to reach me and teach me during the rest of the circle/retreat. I was prepared for deeper insights that could truly affect my life and my work.

Another of my circle/retreat experiences is an example of a self-discovery that had a direct impact on my work. Circle participants were invited to create an art project, a mandala, that could summarize our retreat experience and identify how our work might be influenced by what we had learned and heard from our inner teachers during the event. A mandala represents unity, and can be a model for life itself—a diagram that reminds us of our relationship to the infinite and the world that lies both inside and outside, of ourselves.

I find art projects very intimidating. Even in a college art class, my attempts to cut brittle linoleum tile into a beautiful mosaic, turned out to be a mess of glue globs, ragged, uneven squares and an outline of a Madonna that bore no resemblance to a woman wearing a veil and holding a child. These memories are always grounds for internal shivers. However, as I sat in my chair and felt my feet on the floor and my hands on my lap, I became more grounded and positive. I felt love for myself and everyone in the room; in other words, I was consciously holding space, an important element of a retreat setting. When I finally got up to go to the art resource table and select my mandala supplies, I felt confident and hopeful about an artistic expression of my retreat experience, even though I had no idea what I would actually do.

I instinctively passed by the watercolors, inks, colored pencils and other drawing materials. I truly knew I would not be able to execute anything meaningful using those tools. Just looking at them renewed my feelings of foreboding! As I approached the magazine pages that were placed all around several tables, a sense of willingness filtered over me, and my enthusiasm surged. I was drawn to many pages, mostly to colors and to scenes of lakes, trees, and cityscapes. Picking up a scissors and some glue, and a few colored buttons, I found an open spot at a worktable. Again, I sat for a few minutes with my hands on my lap, my feet flat on the floor, opening my heart to ideas and to inspiration.

After a few minutes, I found myself picking up the scissors and cutting into magazine pages. Colors began to arrange themselves around the outside of the circular cut paper, roughly 9 inches in diameter. The colors became hues of a varied sky, then a few lakes blended into the sky along with a cityscape and and a grassy area, and before I knew it, the paper's space was filled with color and scenes of my home state of Minnesota. Suddenly, it became clear to me what was needed. I found magazine pages with varied shades of red and cut them into heart shaped pieces, then fashioned them into a circle. My heart beating a little faster, I then connected the red shapes with arrows and described the scenario as "hearts holding hands across the State of Minnesota". Just like that, my inner wisdom spoke to me and my new path became clear; I needed to bring together people in Minnesota who were facilitators trained in the the work of Parker Palmer, and find ways to work together to facilitate retreats. Together, we could bring strangers into a retreat setting and support a dialogue that could help to "Heal the Heart of Democracy", the theme of the current retreat experience (and of Parker Palmer's latest book).

For some time, I had been unsuccessfully seeking others in the state who were trained facilitators, and so when it came time to share in a small group, what our art project expressed, I invited the retreat facilitator to sit with me. When I explained my "mandala", she immediately and enthusiastically responded, "I can help you". She did help me by connecting me with amazing resources. She introduced me to people who could connect me and she talked to people about me and recommended me as a facilitator. Ever since that moment of self expression and commitment, all the resources I need have been coming to me as I need them. I met a person who was in a book group reading Healing the Heart of Democracy. I met people who were interested in similar work. I met people who were interested in organizing circles of trust. I was invited to sit on a Foundation that was interested in circles of trust for teachers. My experience of following up on the work is similar to that of doing the art project; when I stay grounded and and listen to myself, and remain in touch with my commitment and with the needs of others, when I hold space, and when I have the courage to be "in there" everything I need to support others, comes to me, bit by bit. I meet people who are interested in my work. I find new people who connect me with others who are interested in healing the heart of democracy and in having me facilitate circles of trust.

Similar to my own experience, most participants begin to experience changes in attitudes towards themselves, their families, and their work. Changed attitudes lead to changed behaviors. The institution's investment in the hearts of their employees yields employees who rediscover their vocations and recommit themselves to the institution's success.

Voluntary participation in circles is essential, to genuinely support individuals, and circles need to be surrounded by a leadership that truly supports "heart" and being true to one's self. In addition, the inner work in community described in my story, is supported by the "rules" of retreats, held in eleven Touchstones; the touchstones help to create a safe space for participants.

Guidelines for a Circle of Trust/Retreat

A circle of trust is a community of like minded persons who use dialogue about a poem, story or song that prompts the ability to listen to one's own inner wisdom (think heart). Renewal and Wholeness circles, in addition to being completely voluntary, use very special guidelines to support a safe space for reflection and self exploration within community. The particular guidelines used in circle settings are eleven Touchstones. Touchstones help to make this retreat experience different from the usual corporate experience where people are mandated to learn a new technique or skill to improve productivity. The Touchstones shared in this chapter have been honed and adapted from those developed by Parker Palmer. As you read this set of norms, you can see how, abiding by them, can help people trust it is safe to speak from their heart without reprisal.

Years ago, I found a definition of dialogue that made so much sense to me. The definition addressed tone when speaking and listening. When speaking, dialogue suggests speaking from the heart using I, reflecting before speaking, being vulnerable and taking a risk, sharing essence not ego, and speaking to connect heart to heart without judgement, rather than to disagree or disconnect. When listening, dialogue encourages listening fully, honoring every comment, staying open, becoming larger not smaller, and being at peace with silence. Interrupting, making someone wrong, giving advice and trying to change someone else's point of view are anathema in dialogue. These suggestions for dialogue are fully embraced in the Touchstones used in retreats. In essence, dialogue is the format for interaction, not decision making or persuasion. Touchstones may be something participants might want to take back to work and implement. One college president, for example, kept copies of the Touchstones in the center of his conference room table. Before meetings, he lit a candle to remind people to speak to the center of the room and the Touchstones were read. It is not their primary intention of the Touchstones, however. Touchstones are behaviors that create a safe environment and that increase the likelihood, the inner teachers of participants will speak to their hearts.

Be 100% present. Extending and presuming welcome. Set aside the usual distractions of things undone from yesterday, things to do tomorrow. Bring all of yourself to the work. We all learn most effectively in spaces that welcome us. Welcome others to this place and this work, and presume that you are welcomed as well.

Listen deeply. Listen intently to what is said; listen to the feelings beneath the words. As Quaker writer Douglas Steere puts it, "Holy listening—to 'listen' another's soul into life, into a condition of disclosure and discovery may be almost the greatest service that any human being ever performs for another." Listen to yourself as well as to others. Strive to achieve a balance between listening and reflecting, speaking and acting.

It is never "share or die. You will be invited to share in pairs, small groups, and in the large group. The invitation is completely open. You determine the extent to which you want to participate in discussions and activities.

No fixing. Each of us is here to discover our own truths, to listen to our own inner teacher, to take our own inner journey. We are not here to set someone else straight, or to help right another's wrong, to "fix" what we perceive as broken in another member of the group. Suspend judgment. Set aside your judgments. By creating a space between judgments and reactions, we can listen to the other, and to ourselves, more fully.

Identify assumptions. Our assumptions are usually transparent to us, yet they undergird our worldview. By identifying our assumptions, we can then set them aside and open our viewpoints to greater possibilities.

Speak your truth. You are invited to say what is in your heart, trusting that your voice will be heard and your contribution respected. Your truth may be different from, even the opposite of, what another person in the circle has said. Yet speaking your truth is simply that it is not debating with, or correcting, or interpreting what another has said. Speak from your heart, not to another's heart. This behavior honors the previous speaker's comments without passing judgment. It also avoids introducing defensive feelings that distract from the listening.

Respect silence. Silence is a rare gift in our busy world. After someone has spoken, take time to reflect without immediately filling the space with words. This applies to the speaker as well—be comfortable leaving your words to resound in the silence, without refining or elaborating on what you have just said. This process allows others time to fully listen before reflecting on their own reactions.

Maintain confidentiality. Create a safe space by respecting the confidential nature and content of discussions held in the formation circle. Allow what is said in the circle to remain there.

When things get difficult, turn to wonder. If you find yourself disagreeing with another, becoming judgmental, or shutting down in defense, try turning to wonder: "I wonder what brought her to this place?" "I wonder what my reaction teaches me?" "I wonder what he's feeling right now?"

Practice slowing down. As Thomas Merton and others have cautioned, the pace of modern life can cause violent damage to the soul. By intentionally practicing slowing down, we strengthen our ability to extend non-violence to others—and to ourselves.

When participants read these powerful norms or touchstones out loud, it is a moving and supportive experience. People realize the circle setting is truly a place to speak from their hearts, and when they do, no one is going to react by saying something contradictory and imply the original speaker is wrong or misguided. If an individual has a different thought than someone else, they simply say it to the center of the room, literally to a candle or a flower or group of stones that draw attention to the center of the circle, in true dialogue fashion. After experiencing these touchstones and the content of the retreats, participants describe changes they find themselves making in their personal and work lives. The changes they describe reflect that the Touchstones are being internalized as norms for working and living

Renewal and Wholeness Circles Inspire Change

Circle/Retreat Work Helps Participants to Know Self in a New Way

Work in Renewal and Wholeness Circles recognizes that we are all engaged in learning, leading and serving, no matter what our job title. This work helps participants to deepen understanding of the reality that we serve or we follow 'who we are', our light and our shadow. One retreat participant explained this deepened understanding: "When I first heard about these retreats, I had read Parker Palmer's books, and they spoke very deeply to me about bringing your authentic self to the task. I think many employees in a lot of places feel they have to take on a certain role or persona at work in order to survive. We are so busy, we disconnect from ourselves and from others. We thrash around trying to meet a lot of demands. I don't have anything off my plate that I used to have; I just manage it better, and I think better."

The 'who we are' aspect of exploration in circles resulted in inner growth and confidence among participants. Several people described how getting to know others and having them provide feedback to them changed their lives. A business coordinator related, "Retreats really helped me with validation. They also really helped me with confidence. My peers were helpful in our sessions. They validated me, they would evaluate me, give me feedback, (by asking open and honest questions) and that gave me confidence that I was doing the right thing in the hair-brained ideas I had 'that's pretty good' they said."

A business and computer science teacher was able to divulge very vulnerable information about himself and his shadow side: "I can't really explain, but I'm not afraid any more about students. I'm not unsure, and retreat involvement caused a lot of that to disappear. My relationships with students have changed. I'm not afraid to get on the same plane as students. I don't feel threatened by students any more. We are all the same, and I started communicating with students on a one-to-one basis. I've stopped trying to prove myself to students. I stopped trying to be the best student in the class. I'm working harder now than ever before in preparing for classes. I'm more concerned about students and I love them more than I ever have before."

Yet another instructor revealed, "Retreats have given me confidence that I can cope with situations and there is always another way to handle something."

Circle/Retreat Reflection Increases Organizational Commitment

Authentic living and working proposes reclaiming the reality and power of our inner life while living full and creative lives in service to an organization and to others. A PR person described his new commitment to his organization: "I can hear more clearly what co-workers are saying and be with them as they express themselves, and instead of escalating situations, to diffuse it. As a manager it's really invaluable to know how to diffuse a situation that could become volatile. Basically, it's taking the time, slowing down long enough to hear what people are saying, and making sure they know they are heard."

One person related her new sense of authenticity this way: "Renewal and Wholeness Circles support more authentic behavior, less fear, more trust among co-workers and better working relationships." Another participant revealed: "I understand our organization better, my colleagues and the entire community. It's relieving sometimes to know that similar problems occur everywhere. That helps me learn from others, find strength from them, and appreciating them and being proud of the work I do here." The organization supporting these individuals is surely experiencing renewal as well as individuals.

A civil rights coordinator thought about it from another perspective: "These retreats provide an opportunity to get to know a few people really well. They have been really beneficial to help me connect with people at different (sites). It has helped me get the resources I need. It has helped to build a sense of trust and community. They unite because you get a chance to hear what's going on in other places and see how similar we are rather than different." Inner work in retreat even helps people to get what they need from others in their organization!

Circles assume that each of us has an "inner teacher" or authentic voice that has the capacity to speak with discernment to the hearts of individuals. One mid level leader recounted her experience with discernment, "What (these retreats) say to me is there's a reason we chose (our) field, our vocation, and we need to get in touch with that again. I spend less energy trying to perform than to just be myself. I have a whole new energy I bring to my work. As I work with my clients and my colleagues, I bring a lot of gifts to my work that I had lost track of along the way." Retreat work is the process of creating a quiet, focused and disciplined space in which the noise within us and around us can subside and the voice of the inner teacher can be heard.

Circles are oriented toward listening from the inside out, and they focus on being rather than on doing. The sessions are designed on the assumption that our work life can be guided by reflection, self-knowledge and contemplation as well as by attention to outcomes and productivity. The powers of the heart can liberate institutions to harness the resources of all the people who work in them; who we are as followers or as leaders affects what we do and how we influence those with whom we work. A staff coordinator was truly liberated, in the circle, to speak from her heart and her organization benefits from her ability to influence others in a more integrated manner: "I speak my mind in meetings, I don't tend to REACT as much as I ACT now. I can accept what other people say and take it in context including their intention, because I think about who they are. I've learned to appreciate the authenticity in them as much as in myself." Another participant echoes this thought, "The opportunity to hear other people's stories and create connections has been the most beneficial. It's probably the most productive experience in staff development I've done in fifteen years of being in this organization."

The circles encourage individuals to draw on their own inner resources. One mid-level manager reported, "I don't feel burned out any more. I know when to reflect on myself and take a pause." Spending time with an individual focus while in community provides people with the time to be comfortable drawing on their own needs and desires and at the same time, hearing the voice of others to prepare for work lives of deeper grounding and authenticity. The same manager shared, "When I go to a meeting now and see my colleagues around the table, I know I can speak from my heart. I know I serve a purpose." Another person reflected similar sentiments, "I became very close to my peers. I gained a lot of respect for them. I found out who they were. It turned out they were extremely nice people. When you get close to them and share with them it is remarkable the things that happen."

Circle/Retreat Content Influences Life Content

The method used for this work is sharing poetry, stories, artwork, or song and then engaging in reflective conversation and collective inquiry. Individuals, in community, are encouraged to tell a story around a theme, and then to see their own and others' gifts. Learning to ask open and honest questions assists participants to go deeper toward their own inner guidance and gives an alternative to advice giving and pointing the way for others.

Several participants described the influence of honest and open questions on their work behavior. One person said, "Open and honest questions in our retreats, I really, really found to be valuable. It was a process of learning how to ask open ended questions of others that help them get more in touch with their truth. It's a process that a piece of it can be used in the workforce in that we listen without bias, we listen for their perspective and we help them be part of a solution and help them come to their solutions instead of telling people what to do."

Exposure to poems, artwork and song influenced some teachers to change their approach to teaching students. One such teacher described her transformation: "In the classroom, I actually took poems to the last class of my speaking and listening class. Students took turns reading aspects of the poem. Students began to look forward to it, a celebration at the end. Students started to bring their own poems and songs or they wrote their own poems. It became a ritual in a sense. I found that students were able to share something more creative and poetic and they were part of it. I find myself listening much more to students. Holding them like a bird, just as we learned to hold each other gently in our retreats. I've encouraged them to take on challenges, I'm going to be there to catch you. That's an image I take with me."

An English as a Second Language teacher put it this way: "Retreats have helped me in the classroom in many ways. One thing is I realized I was a creative person and there is nothing wrong with being creative in the classroom. This semester, I'm doing some wild things that are out of the box. I'm not afraid to do that anymore."

Conclusion

The persons quoted above, who have participated in authentic renewal and wholeness circles/retreats, acknowledge major shifts in their feelings about themselves, their colleagues and their organizations. These experiences reflect those of many participants who find themselves more connected to their colleagues and they gain confidence in their competence. Finding new resources within themselves to use in their work, they build trust in themselves and in their workplace as a community, they gain new energy to take to work, and they speak from their hearts at work.

In whatever job was held by the participants cited, each increased their self-confidence, their sense of vocation, creativity, and productivity. The clients of the organization served by these individuals, whether they are students, people engaged with the human resources or community people dealing with public relations, are all receiving service from more authentic and happy individuals who in turn, are creating a more safe and creative environment.

The purpose of staff development is to support employee competence and effectiveness, to build morale in and strengthen the institution, and to ensure excellent service to customers, patients, or students. It doesn't always work. Many people are turned off by the very word retreat, conference, staff development. It is clear from comments of circle of trust participants, that circles help to accomplish these purposes, yet it happens in a way that is deeply satisfying for individual participants and then productive for all areas of an organization.

Conclusions

by *Cynthia Heelan PhD*

From a marketing executive at Citrix Corporation:

"Teamwork is a lot of people doing what I say."

Anywhere we work, we face challenges to our individuality, to speaking from our heart. There are leaders who believe it is true, that teamwork is a lot of people doing what the leader says. Reading the Chapters in this book, we have learned about the courageous experience of soldiers, dancers, doctors, educational leaders and toy creators. Each writer describes some aspect of themselves they had to overcome to be a good leader and team builder. Each author acknowledges the personal growth they moved through, to be fearless enough to listen to the people with whom they work. Each Chapter describes transformation individuals experienced in their chosen occupation, once they were able to bring their own hearts to their work.

We have heard several people who excel in their chosen field describe the creativity, productivity and high morale they witnessed, once they opened their own heart and created a safe space for the hearts of their colleagues. A dance company created movement that awakened joy in both the dancers and the audience. A Vietnam war veteran created space for fellow veterans to speak heart to heart of their pain, to heal and to become more whole. A toy maker learned of the productivity that comes from play. A college president let faculty tell him what they really thought, and morale and enrollment and college creativity increased.

The purpose of this book is to propose that this can be true for any organization. The steps follow one after another, and each step reflects on and strengthens the one before:

The Path to Heart at Work

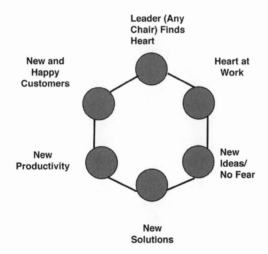

Leader (Any
Chair) Finds
Heart

New and
Happy
Customers

Heart at
Work

New
Productivity

New
Ideas/
No Fear

New
Solutions

- The leader examines himself and his shadow and allows herself to be vulnerable and open at work.
- The leader creates a space for colleagues to also be vulnerable and open at work.
- Workers come together to share their ideas without fear.
- New ideas inspire creative solutions to ordinary and extraordinary problems.

- Productivity increases.
- Sales go up or enrollment increases or colleagues are strengthened or customers are more satisfied or art forms evolve to express ever more innovative ideas
- Each of these activities strengthens and supports one another.
- The leader can be any person sitting in any chair!

Each Chapter author shared a story with the hope that you, the reader could be inspired to keep growing, to create safe spaces in your workplace and in so doing, transform the workplace from one of fear and force to one of openness and love. As Vince Lombardi said, "Teamwork is what the Green Bay Packers were all about. They didn't do it for individual glory. They did it because they loved one another".

List of Resources

Renewal and Wholeness Retreats

Center for Renewal and Wholeness in Higher Education
Richland College
12800 Abrams RD
Dallas, TX, 75343
Phone: 972-238-6242
Email: CRWHE@dcccd.edu

Center for Courage and Renewal
321 High School Road, NE Suite D3 #375
Bainbridge Island, WA 98110-2348
Phone: 206-855-9140
Info@CourageRenewal.org

Appreciative Inquiry Commons

Web: appreciativeinquiry.case.edu

List of References

Almaas, A. H. (1996). *The point of existence.* Berkeley: Diamond Books.

Argyris, C. (1993). *Knowledge for action: A guide to overcoming barriers to organizational change.* San Francisco. Jossey Bass.

Bellah, R.T. (1985) *Habits of the heart: individualism and commitment in American life.* California, University of California Press.

Beattie, M. (1998). *Codependent's guide to the twelve steps.* New York: Fireside.

Bolman, L. G., Deal Terrence E. (1995). *Leading with soul* (First ed.). San Francisco: Jossey Bass.

Cashman, K. (1998). Authentic leadership. *Leadership from the inside out* Accessed July 26, 2005.

Center for Spirituality and Healing at University of Minnesota. http://www.csh.umn.edu/about/home.html, retrieved June 13, 2012.

Citrix Executive. http://www.ahajokes.com/off25.html. Accessed 3/10/12.

Cooperrider, D. L. (1990). *Positive image, positive action: The affirmative basis of organizing in s. Srivastva & d.L. Cooperrider(eds.), appreciative management and leadership:*

The power of positive thought and action in organizations. San Francisco: Jossey-Bass.

Davis, J. (2004) Psychological benefits of nature experiences: research and theory. Boulder, Naropa. http://www.johnvdavis.com/ep/benefits.htm#rel. Retrieved June 16, 2012.

Desjardins, S. (1994) *Meeting on Authenticity and Leadership.* Scottsdale. Phoenix.

Einstein, A. http://thinkexist.com//222006.html. Accessed 3/10/12.

Fritz, R. (1989). *The path of least resistance: Learning to be a creative force in your own life.* New York: Ballantine Books.

Faulkner, A. (2004)*Touchstones,* Center for Renewal and Wholeness, Dallas.

George, B. (2005). *Becoming an authentic leader. http://www.winstonbrill. com/bril001/html/article_index/articles/551-600/article592_body. html*Retrieved May 21, 2005

Ghandi, M. http://www.quotedb.com/quotes/2284. Accessed 3/10/12.

Goethe, J. W. The naked truth quotes: Aspirennies.com. Accessed 1/20/06.

Goff, D. G. (2003). *What do we know about good community college leaders: A study in leadership trait theory and behavioral leadership theory* (Research/Technical Report). Florida: ERIC.

Jaworski, J. (1996). *Synchronicity, the inner path of leadership* (First ed.). San Francisco: Berrett-Koehler Publishers, Inc.

Jones, D. (2010) *Celebrate what's right with the world.* St. Paul. Star Thrower Distribution. STD05S01DVD-0751. Digital Video Disc.

Kijaket al. "Relationship of Blood Sugar Level and Leukocytic Phagocytosis." Journal of Southern California State Dental Associates. (1964):32. Print.

Lombardi, V. http://www.brainyquote.com/quotes/quotes/v/vincelomba151259.html. 3/10/12.

Manning, M. (2005). Creating conversations of consequence: An introduction: Nova Learning.

Manning, M. (1989) *Comments to the Authenticity Group.* Phoenix. Scottsdale Community College.

Mandala Project. http://www.mandalaproject.org/. Accessed April 11, 2012.

Merton, T. (1971) *Contemplation in a world of action.* New York City. Doubleday.

Montaigne, Chapters. Bk. I. Ch. XXV. http://www.bartleby. com/78/628.html. 3/10/12.

Ornish, D. and S.E. Brown et al. (1990). Can lifestyle changes reverse coronary heart disease? The lifestyle heart trial, The Lancet (U.S. National Library of medicine, PubMed). 336 (8708): 129-30. DOI:10.1016/0140-6736(90)91656-U. PMID 1973470. Retrieved July 9. 2012.

Palmer, P.J. (1979) *In the belly of a paradox. A celebration of the contradictions in the thought of thomas merton.* Pennsylvania. Pendle Hill Pamphlet.

Palmer, P. J. (1998). *The courage to teach: Exploring the inner landscape of a teacher's life* (1st ed.). New York: Jossey-Bass.

Palmer, P.J. (1998) *Comments to the Conference on Education as Transformation: religious pluralism, spirituality of higher education,* Wellesley College, Massachusetts.

Palmer, P. J. (2000). *Let your life speak* (First ed.). San Francisco: Jossey Bass.

Palmer, P. J. (2004). *A hidden wholeness: The journey toward an undivided life* (First ed.). San Francisco: Jossey Bass.

Palmer, P.J. (2011) *Healing the heart of democracy: the courage to create a politics worthy of the human spirit.* San Francisco. Jossey-Bass.

Perez, C.J.Pennington, T.S. (2004). *Formation Experience in the Classroom and the Office.* Kansas City. Metropolitan Community Colleges of Kansas City, MO

Pollan, M. (2009). New York. Penguin Books.

Redford, R. (Writer) (2000). *The legend of baggar vance.* USA.

Ringsdorf, W.M. et al. "Sucrose, Neutrophilic Phagnocytosis and Resistance to Disease." Dental Survey December (1976): 46-48. Print.

Riso, D. R. H., Russ. (1999). *The wisdom of the enneagram* (189 ed.). New York: Bantam Books.

Rumi, http://thinkexist.com/quotation/out/340806.html. Accessed 3/10/12.

Sanchez, A. et al. "Role of Sugar in Human Neutrophilic Phagoscytosis." American Journal of Clinical Nutrition November (1973): 26. Print.

Sarton, M. http://www.breakoutofthebox.com/now.htm. Accessed 3/10/12.

Scharmer, C. Otto. (2009)*Theory u: leading from the future as it emerges.* San Francisco. Berrett-Koehler.

Schenk, C. (2004). Energy body workshop: Christine Schenk Technique.

Schenk, C. (2005). *Me and myself.* Hamburg, Germany, Oiri Herstellung: Books on Demand GmbH, Norderstedt.

Senge, Peter; Scharmer, C. Otto; Jaworski, Joseph; Flowers, Betty Sue; (2004) *Presence: human purpose and the field of the future.* Cambridge: Society for Organizational Learning, Inc.

Sinetar, M. (1988). *Elegant choices, healing choices.* Mahwah. Paulist Press.

Shambala Institute. *What guides us.* http://ncdd.org/rc/item/2629. Accessed 5/5/2006.

Shugart, S. (2000) *Keynote address at the international chair academy conference.* Dallas.

Tannen, D. (1990) *You just don't understand: men and women in conversation.* New York. Ballantine Books.

Ungar, L. *Camus lilies.* http://www.panhala.net. Retrieved August 29, 2012.

Wheatley, M. and Kellner Rogues, M. (1999) *A Simpler Way.* San Francisco. Koehler